Time Mana
& Techniques

Learn the most important time management skills
for personal life and career success.

Raymond Le Blanc

Table of Contents

Prologue

"Ever since the invention of time (to be more precise reading of time), people have tried to find ways to make the most out of every second. Some people do that efficiently, whereas other people feel they lose time quite frequently.

Time is a valuable commodity, unless your name is Marty McFly (Back to the Future) and time travelling is something you do regularly. Most of us can only spend a second one time, and many of us cannot remember what we did exactly 7 minutes and 29 seconds ago.

With modern day being extremely hectic, people try to manage time. But how can you manage time, when time itself cannot be contained. How we plan our time to be spent is more realistic. Since this book is about making better use of your time, and not about linguistics, I will conform to the term time management.

You might have tried many strategies to better manage your time at work & with your family. Some of those strategies could include a planner, schedule, agenda, or even a personal secretary. These standard methods have been proven to work, but like every strategy, they can be significantly improved. That is where Raymond Le Blanc can give you a helping hand, as this book contains numerous strategies you probably have never heard of.

As with almost all skills, you need to understand first what your current level of performance is. In this case, you want to know how well you currently manage time. This book contains a self-assessment you can do to see how you are currently doing. When completed honestly, you get a good sense of your time management. That can be used to develop further skills by using any of the strategies detailed in other chapters.

When the author asked if I wanted to write a prologue for his book, I was a bit hesitant, as there is already so much written about time management. After he introduced some of the techniques, I wanted to experiment a little bit, so therefore I tried a few of the techniques myself. The first one was the Pomodoro technique. I used the technique while working on a project, and was amazed how easy it was to get to a result much faster than before. What I liked was that Le Blanc not only introduced the technique, but also explained some of the background, as well as why it works.

Another technique I was already familiar with was the 80/20 rule, and I was happy to see this great rule explained in this book.

Besides a variety of strategies, this book also assists you in staying focused and motivated. One of human's biggest fears is anxiety for not having done what we wanted, or regret about what we have done in life. When it is time for reflection for all of us, we must be content with how we shaped our existence, and how we spent our time.
Having lost time with our family due to heavy workload might be an excuse at times, but it will feel as a terrible loss when the end of time is coming closer.

Start shaping your schedule, reinvent "family quality time", and teach your children that doing one thing really well is better than doing multiple things only half in the same time.

Just by slowing down our days we can save some valuable moments, or at least stand still to enjoy these.

Learn about time, identify your own time weakness, and then start to implement some of the strategies from this book you like best. They have worked for many before you, and should work for you, too. At first, you might spend a bit more time when trying some of the strategies out, which is fine. Your new management strategies have to become your habits, rather than your tools.

Time is the same for everyone. How each of us spends the time is significantly different. Start managing your time, as it will save you time to do things you never had time for…"

Jocelyn Braunn

About The Book

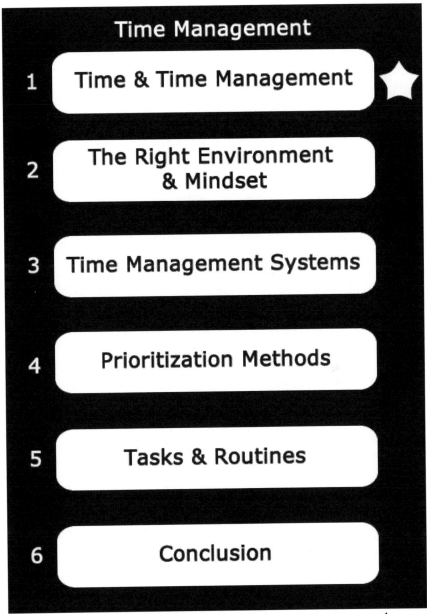

Time Management

1. Time & Time Management
2. The Right Environment & Mindset
3. Time Management Systems
4. Prioritization Methods
5. Tasks & Routines
6. Conclusion

Discover proven time management techniques to turn around every area of your life—at home or at work.

Engaging and down-to-earth author Le Blanc walks you step by step through practical time management techniques to enable you to reach previously unreachable dreams and goals.

You will quickly learn how to use this books information for your own success.

Time Management will help you:

1.   Implement habits as a key to success

2.   Watch your dreams become reality

3.   Achieve more

4.   Be more concentrated and learn better and faster

5.   Increase your pride and satisfaction

6.   Increase focus and work more result driven

7.   Increase your motivation to achieve

8.   Save at least one hour a day and enjoy more free time

9.   Stay motivated, focused and balanced

10.   Cure yourself of the fear of failure

11.   Streamline your communication

12.   Be in control of actions, deadlines and projects

13.   Turn defeat into victory

14.   Experience less stress and more peace of mind

15.   To get more done on time and improve memory

16.   Improve your self-confidence

17.   Drive yourself forward with focus

18.   Stop looking for things and start finding things

19.   Be the best you can be

20.   Revitalize your life

Author Raymond Le Blanc has helped countless people with his easy-to-understand self-management techniques.

Preface

After finishing university as an economist and accepting my first post, I married, made a career and raised children.

Always too many things to do and too little time to do them all.

Having been diagnosed with and treated for a severe panic disorder, I decided to take my career down a new path.

After receiving a master's degree in psychology I made the transition from a banker to clinical psychologist and author. I studied time management, goal setting, and self-management and enthusiastically applied this knowledge to other areas of my life. I soon found I had more time for my family and myself.

As a psychologist and NLP coach, I've helped many people cope with their problems of feeling overwhelmed, exhausted, and even defeated.

The approach in this book blends existing ideas with my experience. The valuable techniques I use in this approach are provided in this book. They are the foremost (and easiest!) methods to enable you to make more time for yourself and to achieve your desired goals.

You will certainly become better equipped to live the life that you really want!

Introduction

We heap our daily schedules full of activities. Despite timesaving conveniences like cell phones, computers and the Internet, we rarely have enough time for our work, our families, friends, or ourselves. So many activities daily demand our attention that it can be difficult to make plans, even if those plans would ease our burdens down the road.

We are busy, but are we productive with our time or happy with the way we spend it?

Many people fail to achieve what they want and what they dream of, simply because they haven't yet discovered the secrets of goal setting and time management.

Managing your time and setting goals are interwoven topics. A healthy time-management plan encompasses goal setting. Achieving goals is only possible when the time factor is considered. With the aid of this book, you can learn to free up your time, and accomplish more than you thought imaginable.

Whether you're a newbie to time management or you've delved into similar books on the subject before, this book has a lot to offer you. It goes beyond presenting techniques; it teaches you step by step, page by page, how to achieve what you've only dared to dream of before. That dream is now within your reach.

It's time to go get it.

Throughout this book you will be asked to answer questions that will help you on your way. It would be handy to grab a notebook or a journal (we'll call it a journal, for simplicity's sake) and a pen or pencil (or an electronic equivalent), and keep them within arm's reach.

To make the most effective use of this book, I recommend you read and put into practice just one simple step, only twenty minutes or so each day, to start relieving your stress, reaching for success, and maybe even learning something surprising about yourself.

It's all in here. Enjoy creating the high quality life you desire.

Let the journey begin.

Raymond Le Blanc

Section 1: Time & Time Management

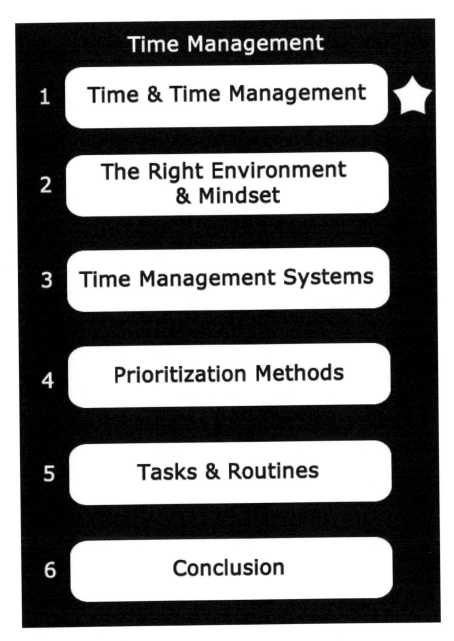

Time Management

1. Time & Time Management

2. The Right Environment & Mindset

3. Time Management Systems

4. Prioritization Methods

5. Tasks & Routines

6. Conclusion

1. What Is Time Management?

"Zhoom! What was that? That was your life, Mate! Oh, that was quick. Do I get another? Sorry, Mate. That's your lot." Basil Fawlty

At this moment you may be faced with some of the following symptoms:

- Multiple to-do lists

- An overflowing mailbox

- Incomplete task lists

- Lots of post-its and reminders

- Postponing tedious tasks

- Difficulties in setting priorities

- Stacks of paper on your desk

- A lack of planning skills

- A lack of concentration

- Always looking for things

- Forgetting things regularly

It doesn't have to be that way!

Time management is absolutely critical to achieving success. Time is the great equalizer: we all have 24 hours in a day. The big question is, 'What do we do with our time?' How do you spend your time? What you choose to do, and with what intensity and focus, will determine whether you have a fulfilling life or a life of disappointment and regret.

Improve your time management skills and you can easily generate an extra hour per day, more likely 2 or 3. What could you accomplish if you created an extra 10-15 hours per week? Spend more time with the people you love? More exercise? Generate a higher income? Play a musical instrument? Finally write that novel?

Time is not renewable and it's way too easy to use it up, only to be gone forever. Wasting time can cost you not only in your time, but in business as well. Your time is a valuable resource that you need to use wisely. You can do several things to make sure you never waste another minute of your time.

So what is time management?

Time management is not about working harder, it's about working smarter. Keeping up with your many tasks can be a scheduling nightmare. Using your time sensibly will give you more time to make better choices in your decisions. When you have to make a decision and you don't have enough time to think about the pros and cons, you may not make a wise choice. It can cost you in time and money.

The key is to plan your time, down to the minute if need be. That way you'll be working smarter, not harder. You'll be able to do all the things that need to be done so you won't have to say any of the following:

- "There is never enough time to do what is important."

- "Other people make too many demands on my time."

- "Given my busy schedule, it's impossible for me to work based on priorities."

- "If you want something done right, do it yourself."

Sounds very familiar, doesn't it? They can all be dealt with because there is always enough time, it's just poorly managed. Too many people needing your time means they are controlling you, so you need to control them and your time. Priorities are important and you need to set time for them and stick to the schedule. Don't let anything interfere with that time. There are many people who can do the same thing you do, you need to delegate those tasks. They may do it their way, but if the results are the same, who cares. It's a trust issue that takes your time -- time that can be spent doing more important things.

You've probably said some of the following:

- "I'm often overworked in my job."

- "I'm much too busy to plan my activities."

Sometimes you just have to bite the bullet and make time to plan your time. That's what time management is all about -- planning your time, so you have more of it. Make a schedule and stick to it, no matter what. You should say, "I should stick to my plan for the day, no matter what happens." If something comes up, set the priority or delegate the task. You'll soon become used to managing your time.

There are some major benefits to managing your time. You won't ever have to say, "I don't have time." You'll be able to find the time once you setup your time schedule. It also helps you make better decisions. What? Studies have shown people who use time management make better decisions. The reason is this: you have more time to think about the pros and cons of a choice before making the decision to act.

You'll also gain valuable flexibility for your time. That's important when a family member calls and needs help. You won't be backed up at work because there's time in your schedule for emergencies.

You really can't say, "I don't have time for your problem right now. I have to work, sorry."

Of course, there's no way you can tell your boss you can't do what he wants without putting yourself into a serious predicament. Time management also gives you confidence in your abilities and makes you look more confident. When you are overworked, you look overworked and harassed all the time. Managing your time takes all that away and gives back confidence, enjoyment in your work, and flexibility with your time.

Not to mention the stress overwork puts on your body. Think about not having a headache first thing in the morning or a tight stomach, or a pain in the neck. Time management is one of the best ways to beat the stress that just makes work harder. The harder you work, the less time you have.

So you gain confidence, time of course, less stress, better decision-making abilities, flexibility with your time, and you lose the feeling of being overwhelmed all the time. There are only benefits for managing your time, there's no down side. Why would you not use time management to improve your life?

Sometimes, the world doesn't give us much time to react with the right choices. You can damage your reputation if you're always canceling appointments or not spending enough time with your clients. The key to managing your time is planning, setting priorities, and delegating. The next time the boss gives you an assignment that isn't in your time management, you'll have time to slip it in, and you won't even notice. After you've done it for a while, you'll wonder why it took you so long to plan out your time.

2. The Value of Your Time

Have you ever taken a look at how you spend your time and how it relates to your energy levels? Every dollar has a definite value, but every hour does not. For example, you may have more value in your time from seven o`clock in the morning to twelve noon, rather than 10 o'clock in the evening to 11 o'clock in the evening. Everyone has a different value on his or her time. Some may put more value in spending 30 minutes reading a bedtime story to his or her child than 30 minutes on work emails. It is a personal choice.

Looking at Your Time in Money Terms

Taking into consideration the value of your time can cause you to have more appreciation for the time that is given to you each day. It may even cause you to use time differently, such as in ways that have more meaning to you. There are two main ways that you can put a dollar value on your time, looking at time from the employer's point-of-view and from your own point-of-view:

What is the cost of one hour of your time at work to your employer?

If you work for someone else, you are costing his or her business more than just your hourly wage. Consider the other benefits you receive, other than your base salary. You may have life insurance, health insurance, dental insurance, long-term care, pension plans, and other retirement benefits. Not to mention paid holidays, sick time, and vacation time – all paid for by the company when you are not even at work.

In addition to these benefits are the equipment you use that cost electricity, the office space you hold that has to be cleaned and maintained, and the supplies that you need to perform your job. These are all benefits that are paid by the employer as part of your employment package. Consider these costs when you perform your job, or when you decide to waste time.

For example, say your monthly gross salary is $2,000. Adding an average 30 percent for other costs brings your salary to $2,600. Divide this by the average hours you work in a month, which is about 160 hours. You cost your employer $16.25 per hour. See the value?

What does an hour cost you?

What if you are self-employed or do contract work on your own time. How do you determine what an hour costs you? Spending your time wisely or wasting time has a direct effect on your income level, so there is no doubt that every hour of your time is very valuable and accounted for. When your income depends on your output, you can easily see the value of your time.

As an exercise, try creating a list of business-related activities that do not directly create income, such as contacting potential clients, paying bills, web research, and cleaning. Using the previous month as your guideline, estimate how many hours you spent on each task. Say each task took 12, 8, 20, and 10 hours respectively.

Let's say you charge $20 per hour for the services, spending a total of 50 hours per month; this equals an income possibility of $1,000. This time may have caused you to spend valuable time away from your family, such as missing trips to the beach or park, or even simple things as watching a family movie together. Understanding the value of your time in dollars can assist you in making wiser choices on how you spend your time. Sometimes it may be cheaper to hire someone else to do the cleaning of your home, so you can spend those hours with your family. It becomes your decision on what is most important to you.

Looking at Your Time beyond Money

Managing your time goes far beyond identifying the monetary value of your time spent on tasks and work. Personal time has much value. You are valuable. You have families, hobbies, special interests, and dreams. If you base your time in this life strictly on the value of money, there may be something that you may have to give up – something that will become missing from your life.

For example, say your child has a school play that he or she wants you to attend, but it is during your work hours. Do you ask for time off or do you worry about the money and work time you will lose? Or say your child is involved in a sporting activity on the weekend, and you are totally exhausted from a hectic week at work; you need to clean the house and wash the clothes. Do you attend the sporting activity or do you worry that your house is dirty? It is your choice, and only you can determine the value of your time beyond its monetary value.

To help put things in better perspective for you, imagine you just found out that you only have three months to live. How would you spend your time? Really think about this. What would you do? What would really matter to you? The answer to this question is what should be the guiding factor in how you live your life.

3. How Are You Doing?

Here's an easy self-test to find out how well your time-management skills are currently developed.

For each of the questions below, give yourself 3, 2, 1, or 0 points, according to the following scoring key:

> If your answer is "always," give yourself 3 points.
> If your answer is "usually," give yourself 2 points.
> If your answer is "occasionally," give yourself 1 point.
> If your answer is "rarely" or "never," give yourself 0 points.

Question / Score

1. Do you think about and plan your day before you start it?
2. Do you write appointments and key tasks in your calendar?
3. Do you keep—and use—a continuing "to do" list?
4. Do you use this "to do" list as a reminder of things you would like to do in the future?
5. Do you group similar tasks together and do them consecutively?
6. Do you use waiting time to handle small tasks?
7. Do you handle the most important tasks of the day when you feel most alert?
8. Do you stop working on a task when you begin to feel stressed or overwhelmed?
9. Do you feel your personal life and professional life are well balanced?
10. Do you keep a simple but well-defined filing system into which you place all loose papers and materials?
11. Do you organize your work tools, such as pens, rulers, phone and computer so they are ready to use the minute you want them?
12. When you enter your office or pick up your mail, do you immediately discard messages and items you don't need?

13. Do you keep reference materials, such as telephone books, rolodexes, and important manuals within arm's reach of your primary work area?
14. Do you have a specific time allotted each day to handle memos, messages, and correspondence?
15. Do you shut your door or engage in quiet time when you must handle detail work?
16. Do you keep a simple time log to systematically access where and how you spend your time?
17. Do you have a good insight in the values you live by?
18. Do you regularly review 90-day goals for your personal and professional life?
19. Do you take time each week to appraise your productivity and discover whether you have completed the goals you set out to accomplish?

Total your points. _____

If your score ranges between 50 and 60, congratulations! You are nearing perfection. There's still room for some improvement though. The following chapters will help you to top things off.

If your score ranges between 40 and 49, good. With some modest improvements in your time-management habits, you can become even more productive each day. After completion of this book you will be able to achieve your goals quickly and have more time for yourself.

If your score ranges between 30 and 39, you're on the right track. You need to make a few easy changes that will enable you to accomplish more and free up time as well. This book will serve as your guide.

If your score is below 25, you've definitely come to the right place. The following chapters can dramatically help you to improve your time management skills and achieve far more than you ever thought possible.

This self-test gave you an indication of how you are currently managing your time. Feel free to take the test again over the coming months so that you can track – and enjoy watching – your progress.

4. Activity Logs

A method you can use to get more detailed insight into how you are using your time is an activity log. An activity log is simply a page or two in your journal where you record how you spend a day's time. When you first use an activity log you may be shocked to see the time you waste!

Memory is a poor guide when it comes to this, as it can be too easy to forget time spent on non-core tasks. Do you have any idea how much time you spend eating lunch? Reading junk mail? Talking to colleagues? Doing the laundry? Or fetching a missing ingredient at the grocery store?

Activity logs can also help you to track changes in your energy, alertness and effectiveness throughout the day. A lot of people discover they work at different degrees of effectiveness throughout the day as their energy level fluctuates. Your effectiveness may vary based on: blood sugar levels, routine distractions, the length of working without a break, discomfort, stress, or other causes.

Assignment

Keep an activity log for two days to better understand how you spend your time and when you perform at your best. Choose two days which you would consider to be normal days.
In your journal, log your activities, the importance or value of that activity, and how you feel throughout each day. List the start times of each activity and write down a new start time each time you change activities.

Here is an example of an activity log:

Activity Log

Time - Activity - Description - Duration - Value (high, medium, low) - How I feel
8:05 - prepare breakfast - 20 - high - tired

8:25 - read newspaper - 10 - medium - tired
8:35 - drive to work - 35 - high - flat
9:10 - fetch coffee + greet coworkers - 10 - low - flat
9:20 - open + check mail + start computer- 5 - medium - flat
9:25 - interruption coworker - 10 - low - flat
9:35 - check mail - 5 - medium - flat
9:40 - start working on important report - 10 - high - alert
9:50 - telephone interruption - 10 - low - flat

While you do not have to state your mood for each activity, try to establish a pattern by listing at least every hour how you feel: alert, flat, tired, energetic, and so on. The more detailed your log, the easier it will be to see patterns emerge.

Assignment
After two days, analyze your daily activity log. You may be alarmed to see the amount of time you waste doing low-value jobs. You may also notice that you feel energetic in particular parts of the day, and flat in other parts. Much of this can depend on the rest breaks you take, the times and amounts you eat, and quality of your nutrition.

Also take into consideration the energy drainers and energy gainers. Could an energy drainer or gainer be something you ate? A conversation you had? Something you did? An interruption? The activity log gives you a basis for experimenting with these variables.

Understand your peak times. If you are a morning person, get up at the crack of dawn and get jobs done. Recognize your most productive times, and schedule your most important tasks within those times.

Your analysis should help you determine time you can free up during your day. Gain that extra time by applying one of the following actions to as many time-wasting activities as possible:

- Reduce the time spent on legitimate personal activities such as making coffee. Take turns with your team member to do this—it saves time and strengthens team spirit.

- Try to lessen the number of times a day you switch between kinds of tasks. For example, read and reply to e-mails in blocks only once in the morning and once in the afternoon.

- Schedule your most challenging tasks for the times of day when your energy is highest. That way your work will be better and it should take you less time.

- Cut out jobs that your employer shouldn't be paying you to do. These may include tasks that someone else in the organization should be doing, possibly at a lower pay rate, or personal activities such as sending non-work related e-mails or checking your social media.

5. *Eliminate Your Energy Drainers*

Another benefit of gaining insight in your energy level fluctuation is that it will enable you to discover energy drainers and eliminate them.

Assignment

Log your emotional energy for one day (an example follows). Try to identify what causes your emotional energy to remain level, what causes your emotional energy to fall and what causes your emotional energy to raise. When your emotional energy is between two levels, try to identify where the strongest energy is. This log will enable you to pinpoint emotional energy drainers.

Energy level survey

Time	Energy Level	Causes
09:00-11:00	High	I feel in shape and confidant.
11:00-13:00	High – Middle	I still feel relatively good but a little annoyed because of so many interruptions.
13:00-15:00	Low	I feel ashamed because I failed an important exam.
15:00-17:00	Middle	I slowly realized I did not pay enough attention preparing for the exam and I am confident I will pass next time. Plus I have great plans for tonight.

Most of us spend most of our time in the middle energy level. In this example the many interruptions between 11:00-13:00, and the fact that the energy level reported is slipping could be an indication that interruptions drain your energy. This log shows us temporary emotional energy drainers. But what if instead it revealed a persistent low energy level? That could be a true concern.

When your energy continuously runs low over longer periods of time, there are usually multiple issues and problems causing this. These feelings can be serious energy drainers.

If you find yourself stuck in a state of low energy level you might want to consider help from others to tackle the issues that could be causing you emotional exhaustion and might be holding you back.

If you have a persistent low or middle emotional energy level, set a goal to learn more about your emotional level and then set another goal to lift yourself to a higher level. By doing so you will eliminate debilitating energy drainers and have more and better quality time with which to achieve, succeed, and excel. Being able to define the important areas of yourself, and to take control of the way your life is spent, is a potent energy booster in itself.

—— Sidebar ——
Energy drainers can prevent us from living a healthy and fulfilled life. These energy drains can be found in several areas of life.

Health and Well-Being
Exercise
Sleep
Diet
Substance abuse

Relationships
Neglecting some people
Say yes instead of no too often
Stress and conflict
Anger, hurt and guilt
Forgiveness
Control

Career
Work demands
Fun
Stress

Finances
Expenses
Income

Debt
Bills

Living Environment
House
Neighborhood
Clutter
Maintenance
----

6. Your Personal Prime Time

Learning time management is easier than you may think. In grade school we learned tactics that helped us reach simple goals. From our parents we learned basic time management. If you feel you are running a tight shift, it simply means that it is time to learn extra skills to get ahead.

We have our own rhythm of when we can be more productive, and times when we are less productive.
Simply by knowing your energy pattern you can conserve your energy and steer clear of a burnout. The pattern associated with ideal energy management is one where you are wholly engaged and using all of your resources for greatest productivity, followed by a period of intense recovery where you recover all your energy for the next job ahead.

The first new skill? Use your personal prime time.

Successful time management starts with: making the most of your time! To do so we must make a distinction between prime time and availability time.

Prime Time

Your prime time, which you may have discovered with the use of your activity log, is the time during which you are most energetic and efficient.

Reduce interruptions during your best working hours. You can carry out twice as much in one quiet hour as in two regular hours of frequent interruptions.

If you haven't yet discovered your prime time, answer these questions: At what hours of the day do I work best? When do I achieve the greatest results?

Try to think of the time of the day where you usually accomplish more than at the other hours of your day. Try to discover a pattern in these highs and lows. We function on different biological clocks. Some people feel most energetic and do their best work early in the morning. Others wake up and get moving slowly, with top efficiency in the late afternoon. Still others are night owls who perform their work most easily in the middle of the night.

So now that you know your prime time, how do you make the most of it? Plan to spend it on your creative thinking and most demanding jobs whenever possible. Doing so will enable you to excel at your most important tasks, and allow you to accomplish them as quickly as possible.

If you feel you have more energy during the morning, set your important tasks during this time and schedule the less important ones in your less productive hours. You can also set your big and difficult tasks during this time to get productive results and do the short and simple tasks during your down time.

The main element to effective energy management is always to set up routines in your daily life that promote periods associated with heavy involvement followed by recovery.

Availability Time

Your availability time is when you need to be available to be with others. For example, busy executives must schedule time to meet with office personnel, managers, production workers, and others under their supervision. To make the most of your prime time, schedule your availability time around your periods of top efficiency.

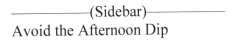
————————(Sidebar)————————
Avoid the Afternoon Dip

You are probably familiar with the afternoon slump – the lazy drowsy feeling after lunchtime. Your energy levels go down. It's hard to focus and think. Your motivation is at a complete low.

If you are feeling lifeless in midday, consider these questions:

- Did I eat any breakfast today?
- What did I have for breakfast?
- What did I have for lunch?

Your answers may give a hint to your problem. A mug of coffee while on the road for breakfast along with a chocolate bar from the dispenser for lunch may provide you with the caffeine and sugar you need to get started, but not the durable energy you need to keep going.

There are several preventive measures you can take.

Tips:

- Get enough sleep. Make sure you're getting to bed at a sensible hour. A good night's rest will put your mind at ease and let you wake up refreshed and ready to start the day. After a terrible day of stress and headaches you can always go to bed and awaken to a bright new sunny tomorrow
- Drink more water. Being slightly dehydrated reduces your concentration levels
- Don't overdo things at lunch. Have lunches that include at least three of the four food groups. And avoid overeating too. All that extra digestion your body has to do takes energy away from your brain.

To climb out of your afternoon dip, try these measures:

Tips:

- Open a window. You'll find that it's a lot easier to stay alert when you're cool. The fresh air will keep you relaxed.
- If you have faced the computer for a long time, stand up and divert your attention for a while to avoid destroying your precious eyesight. Also, let your body enjoy, relish

and breathe in fresh air. Move around. Go for a brisk walk or better yet, find the staircase in your office building and do five or six flights to get your blood pumping and your body warmed up. Ideally, make a walk part of your regular routine, either during your lunch hour or during an afternoon break.

- Get fueled. If you weren't fortified well at breakfast and lunch, you need to take a moment and have a snack. Good options include fresh fruit, trail mix with nuts, or whole-wheat crackers with string cheese.
- Clean your desk and clear out your email inbox. Both are relatively mindless tasks that don't require great amounts of concentration or clear thinking, and both will leave you feeling more energized because you'll have accomplished something visible as well as having reduced clutter.
- Sit back and relax for fifteen minutes.

Section 2: The Right Environment & Mindset

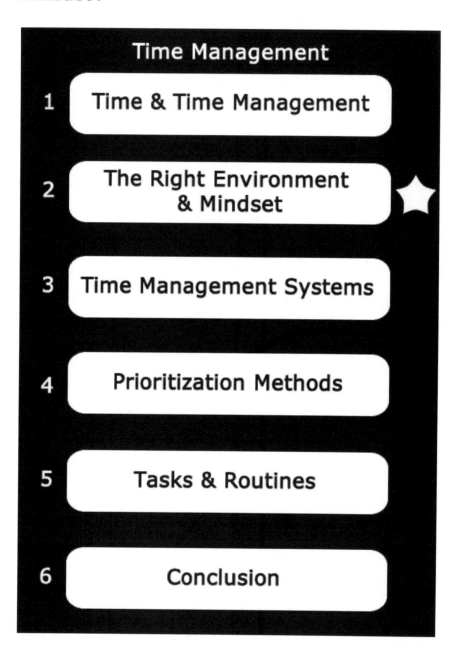

7. A Supportive And Effective Environment

Time management literature often stresses tasks related to the creation of an environment conductive to real effectiveness. They refer to issues such as the benefit of a tidy office or home to unleashing creativity, and the need to protect "prime time".

These strategies include principles such as:

- Getting Organized

- Protecting Your Prime Time

- Motivational Emphasis

- Dealing With Procrastination

Writers on time management often focus on creating an environment for effectiveness.
This literature also focuses on overcoming chronic psychological issues such as procrastination and lack of motivation.

These will be the topics of this section of this book.

8. Get Organized

An organized work space is a must for using your time well each day. When you are spending time looking for a pen, a specific file, or misplaced document, you are wasting precious time. In addition to wasting time, you are more likely to increase your stress level, which can directly affect your ability to concentrate on work that needs to be done.

Clutter can cause you to spend so much time searching for items that your clear focus on your task suffers.

You may ask if organizing takes too much time. Well, it doesn't have to. Maybe in the beginning it will take some devoted time to organize your work space, but once you have it organized, maintaining it becomes easier. After each work day, it may take an average of 15 minutes to reorganize your desk for the next day, but it is time well spent. Consider spending 30 minutes to look for items in comparison to 15 minutes of organization. Organizing is worth the time. Here are some simple suggestions:

- Document Filing and Naming
  Naming and color-coding your files can greatly improve the organization of your information of both physical and digital files. Noting the draft number on a document helps in identifying consistent versions in the event you want to go back to review an earlier draft. Also including the date that the document was created can also be beneficial when searching for past documents.

- Storage Space
  Always have at least 50 percent more storage space than you think you will actually need. This is a great way to de-clutter your work space and keep other items neatly stored for future reference, if needed. You may consider investing in filing cabinets and bins that are affordable and will do the job in giving you more work space. Having storage

items in an easy accessible place, away from your work space frees your space from unnecessary items.

- De-Cluttering
  Begin with the obvious items that you don't need or don't use. Throw it away or donate it to someone else or to a local charity. Items that take up space just confuse you into thinking that all that items are important, when in actuality it could just be junk.

- Remove the Trash
  Don't let trash build up in your workspace. Have it removed at the end of each day to maintain a healthy and clean environment.

- Filing
  File all papers that you have designated folders for. If there is no designated folder, create one immediately so that there are no lose papers hovering on your work desk.

- Recycle
  Any unwanted magazines or reading material should be recycled for others to enjoy, or else thrown away. The ones that you want to keep should be organized on a bookshelf or magazine rack.

- Everything Needs a Home
  Everything, from cell phones, keys, and personal belongings should all be placed in an appropriate location and not scattered over your desk. By leaving personal and work belongings all over your work space, it not only looks disorganized, but you will most likely waste time trying to find your things.

- Items that Should Remain on Your Desk
  Company phone lists, calendars, and items that you are currently working on should be the only items on your work desk. At the end of each week, toss out any irrelevant

items, organize your desk for the next week, and file all lose papers.

- Organize your Files
  Take a portion of one of your work days to organize all the files you have in your filing cabinets and drawers. Place the files in the order that is most beneficial to your work style. Label all new files to match your current filing system, so it can be easily located when needed.

- Organize your Computer Files
  Your computer files should be organized according to subject area that will be easily retrievable when needed. Save files under common areas related to your work for ease of locating.

- Important Documents
  Important documents should be filed together in a locked file cabinet. These documents should not be mixed with general items, as it should always be kept in a safe place.

- Create a File for New Ideas/Projects
  Keep a separate file of your currently working documents and projects that you will most likely need on a daily basis. Projects should be separated into different files, if you are working on more than one at the same time. As always, ensure that all files are labeled properly.

- Get colorful.
  Purchase file folders with different colors to represent different topics or subject areas that you work on. For example, green folders could represent financial matters, red folders could be for urgent matters or projects, and yellow folders could be for miscellaneous items.

- Use tickler files.
  This is a system of filing for papers that you use often that have regular deadlines. For example, the information is

kept in files according to due dates in a separate filing area. Each day you check what is due or needs to be done for that day. There are many different styles of tickler systems. There is a 45-file system, where the present month is organized by using 31 tickler files. It can also be organized monthly and by the year.

- Task filing.
  You can use a system similar to the tickler file. Create a file folder for each day of the month. This allows you to easily schedule tasks for each day. Each morning you can pull the file for the day and review the day's tasks. A 45-pocket filing system can work great for this system.

- Bill filing.
  You can use a system similar to your work task filing system. If bills are due on the 20th, for example, you can place it in the day 15 folder to give you enough warning to pay your bills on time. This system makes it virtually impossible for you to miss important deadlines.

- Year filing.
  This type of system is for items that don't need to be looked at until the following year, such as tax information.

There are many creative ways to create your files in relation to the above guidelines, but remember, only use what works best for you.

Organizing your Home Work Spaces

You may also have a work space at home for your home business and managing of your personal important papers and tasks. Little time should be spent looking for bills and items for children's sports and schooling when your home is organized. Here are some tips to organize your home for efficiency:

- In the kitchen, keep your table and countertops clear of papers and items that should be placed in appropriately assigned places. Having a clean and organized space will make you more efficient. Kitchen drawers should also be organized according to usage. For example, pencils and pens should not be placed with forks and spoons!

- Utilize a decorative box or small storage bin to use for your multi-purpose items that really have no designated place for storage. You can also use a box to gather miscellaneous items from around the house when cleaning, and then place items in its proper place.

- Clean out your belongings. Every three months go through your belongings and keep only the things that you use regularly, and donate or throw away items that you no longer use or haven't used in months. To make a decision to get rid of items, ask yourself when was the last time you used it and if you truly will use it in the future. Once you clean out these items, you can organize whatever is left.

- Avoid buying bulky items. You home should have enough space for easy use and movement, and not be overcrowded with large appliances or office equipment.

- Make the temperature just right. Temperature is a factor that could either irritate or motivate a person to work. Temperature should be just right and the senses should be tempered with pleasant stimuli during work. Not having to stop work to pull on a sweater or to cool off with trips to the water cooler allows you to focus on your tasks.

The best way to determine how well you are organized is by how good you feel. There is calmness and lack of anxiety that is felt when the environment you work and live in is clean, comfortable, and well-organized - a place free from things piling up and overwhelming you.

For additional resources on organizing your home, you may read Eliminate Chaos: The 10-Step Process to Organize Your Home &

Life by Laura Leist. This is a system that is user-friendly in assisting you to organize every area of your home, from the kitchen to the children's rooms. For additional tips on organizing your space at work, read Organizing Your Space, Revised Edition: A Guide to Personal Productivity by Odette Pollar. This book discusses various ways of avoiding paper backlogs, managing your desk, and keeping a clutter free desk.

9. Mind Mapping

Many people have great ideas but lack the skills to put them on paper. Mind mapping is a very powerful tool that has helped many people piece together scanty pieces of information, thus helping them increase their productivity. It encourages the solving of complex problems by coming up with a way in which they relate to each other.

A mind map is generally very different from the way people usually take notes. It represents a graphical representation of a complex problem. Mind maps are drawn to represent information in the simplest possible ways. Just like how the brain naturally works. It is scientifically proven that mind mapping engages the brain thus making it more productive and able to come up with different solutions to many problems. It further enables one to subdivide a complex problem into several modules which interrelate. For a mind map to be good it has to have the overall subject subdivided into smaller units which then relate to each other. Whenever a new idea surfaces it is very easy to integrate it into the mind map and relate it to the others.

Benefits of Mind Maps

There are many benefits associated to using mind maps. Some of the major benefits include that one can **effortlessly** summarize information in a way that it can easily be understood, it is a very strong tool for solving complex problems and it can be used to present a problem showing how the different sources of information relate.

For many people learning how to use a mind map for brainstorming and goal setting will be an exciting expansion of their current knowledge and skill set. In addition it can also be a better and easier way for you to take notes and study many other subjects as well.

For others it may first appear to be a bit of a challenge, but the good news is that once you learn more about them you will see just how easy and natural they can be to work with.

What Is A Mind Map

Basically a mind map is simply a visual diagram consisting primarily of :

* pictures or images which should be used to represent your key topics, ideas or tasks.

* keywords or keyword phrases that also capture the essences of a topic, idea or task.

* circles and line which can be one or multiple colors. These contain the images and show the connection or flow between topics, tasks or ideas.

When properly constructed a mind map can be used as a very effective whole-brain learning tool for generating, capturing and organizing ideas and information.

Images are associated with right brain holistic functions and keywords are associated with your left-brain analytical functions.

You should also use different color pens or markers which help to stimulate your creativity and imagination which are right-brain functions.

Mind maps are more of a free form way of creating a to do list or capturing ideas without having the constraint of needing to have everything listed in a sequential order.

This allows you to focus more of your attention on the task of capturing useful and relevant ideas as apposed to worrying about what order everything needs to be in.

Prioritizing and organizing the task is done in a separate step from capturing all of the ideas and needed information.

How To Use A Mind Map for brainstorming and goal setting

The good thing about doing brainstorming and goal setting together is that you are combining one creative activity with another, which works out really well. Here is a simple 4 step process that you can follow:

Step 1.) Start with your goal – Write it in the middle of a sheet of paper if possible create a picture or symbol to represent it and then circle it. On the outside of the circle you should write a keyword that accurately represents your topic.

Step 2.) write down (in a free style form) other thoughts or ideas that come to mind that will be needed or supportive in achieving your goal. Circle them and draw a connection between them and your goal.

Step 3.) You now need to add any sub task that may needed to be completed for any task that will require a preceding action. For example if you are creating a mind map for starting a business, your goal may be to become financially independent.

Prior to achieving that goal there will be quite a few major and minor milestones to reach along the way. After you have written down the major ones (like get your equipment and have your product created) you would then list the smaller tasks (like find the best vendor or get the best pricing, etc...)

Step 4.) Once you have all of the items needed, you can then organize them and make sure that everything is in a logical order.

In many cases you will find that working through this process will not only help you organize your thoughts and see the big picture but it will also help to embed your goal and plans into your subconscious mind where they can take on a power of their own.

Recommended tools to use for mind mapping include :

+ A White board

+ A Notepad or sheet of paper

+ Software programs or Mind mapping Apps

10. Evernote

Evernote is a suite of services and software specially designed for archiving and note taking. Each note can have its own attachments and can be sorted into folders. Moreover, they can be exported, searched, tagged and edited. Evernote supports several operating systems, including Mac OS, Microsoft Windows, Android and IOS. This modern software reached more than 11 million users so far since its launch in June 2008. Evernote is available in both paid and free versions. However, the second one is more restricted and has a certain usage limit.

How to Save Time Using Evernote

In our modern world, spending less time doing daily tasks has become a necessity. We are extremely busy, so we look for new alternatives to help us save time. Evernote has been found to be extremely helpful when it comes to save more of your precious time, which can be used for other tasks. The following ways to use Evernote are extremely popular today, allowing both business people and employees to be more productive and in the same time keep their life organized:

- Access it from everywhere: this is probably one of the best advantages of Evernote, and also the best feature for better time management. Your laptop, desktop, smartphone or even tablet can be used to access Evernote fast and securely. Take advantage of all the options available and don't limit yourself only to one device.

- Take pictures of the things you want to remember and upload them to Evernote. By doing this, you will save plenty of time, because a picture is worth a thousand words. Rather than trying to write down a complicated task or description of something, simply take a picture.

- Scan all your notes: if you have paper notes, scan them and upload them to Evernote. This unique software features OCR (Optical Character Recognition), which will allow your handwritten notes to become instantly searchable.

- Use it as your paperless library: if you've had enough of papers and documents that are difficult to find, why not go paperless? With Evernote, you can save plenty of time, because you can file all PDF scans in one place, like a huge online library. You won't need to get up from your chair anymore in order to go and look for a missing document. You will have all you need in one place, stored safely.

- Use Evernote for reference information, even if you know your favorite food brands and the most suitable clothing sizes, sometimes you need to remember the air filter size, the type of tires for your brand new SUV or the model of light bulb needed in your bathroom. Evernote helps you keep all these information at your fingertips, so try to maximize this benefits it offers.

- Save all important registrations and receipts; it is a proven fact that many people just like you and me are unaware of what to do with old receipts. If you have them all stored in your email inbox, you can transfer them at a click of a mouse into your Evernote account. Use Evernote for better time management by storing all your old receipts in one secure place.

- Lists, notebooks and collections: this software is a great place to store all your collections and lists. You can easily store your favorite recipes, movie lists, wine collection or favorite TV shows. Moreover, Evernote has a unique feature that allows you to create shared notebooks, which can be used by both you and your business partner to share common ideas and plans. In addition, you can collect notes, such as prices, schedule and features, of the next vacation you're planning abroad.

- Solutions to various problems: in case you deal with the same problem over and over again, you need to store the solution in a safe place that can be easy to access. This is where Evernote jumps in and proves once again that it's a reliable partner for better time management. It is important to save your solutions if you don't want to solve the same problem multiple times.

11. Time-Saving Tools

There are many time-saving tools that can be utilized on your path to efficiency. These devices are specifically designed to assist you in meeting your goals and accomplishing tasks in an effective manner. Here are some common devices used for time management:

- Computers – Commonly used to send documents and information quickly and manage multiple calendars. Having access to the Internet is also essential for running effective programs that can allow you to share documents instantly and work effectively. E-mail also is a great service in keeping you in constant communication with others in a multiple of ways. Using the auto responder with e-mail lets those trying to contact you, when you will be able to get back to them; thereby, managing your time wisely.

- Cell Phones – With the development of smart phones, this device is commonly used to manage not only calls, but emails and calendars. Managing all these items remotely allows you to keep track of tasks and items that need to be completed. The availability of voicemail is also a means of keeping everyone informed of your availability, as well as allowing the freedom for people to leave messages that you can return according to your schedule.

- Memo Recorder – This device allows you to record ideas or tasks that need to be completed when you remember it. This gives you the means to ensure no idea or task is forgotten, making you even more productive in managing your time.

- Car CD Player – Having a CD player in the car is an excellent way to make the best use of your time – not with music, but with education. You can listen to motivational, inspiring, and various educational CDs for your own personal development.

- iPod or iPad – These devices can be downloaded with audio and/or educational videos and/or recordings, which you can use to improve your skills. They also offer programs that can be used for managing tasks, meetings, and calendars.

- Video Conferencing – Using video conferencing is a way to save time from having to travel distances for a meeting. A meeting can simply be held at your place of work, saving you travel time; time that you can use for other productive tasks.

- Personal Information Manager (PIM) – This is a software application that operates as your own personal organizer for every area of your life, both personal and professional.

You should consider researching the devices that would work best for you and your needs. As finances permit, purchase the devices that will allow you the best in time management. Purchase what will be beneficial to you, and not something that will be too difficult for you to use, or you will end leaving it in a drawer under a pile of other gadgets.

Technology should never be a hindrance to your success in creating and managing your life. You should use devices that will make you more productive, well informed, and reachable. These sophisticated devices can make your life much easier to manage.

12. Protect Your Prime Time

Protect your prime time by protecting yourself from information overload, demands by others and by delegating/outsourcing when possible.

13. E-mail

E-mail has helped save a lot of time and money for many people. Instead of the old-fashioned snail mail, more individuals rely on e-mail to get their messages across faster, cheaper, and more conveniently.

However, there is a downside to using e-mail as a means of communication. Many people check their e-mail frequently throughout the day, thereby hampering their productivity. Some have become addicted to e-mail and spend hours reading and replying.

Below are tips to make e-mail work for you.

Check your e-mail twice a day, maximum. Suitable times would be first thing in the morning (to take care of urgent matters) and at the end of your work day (to catch up with last-minute concerns). Often when I log into my mail account I end up with more work on my plate -- and because most of us are conditioned so, we start replying to them at the expense of the duties we were just taking care off. Rather than actively sticking to your agenda, email lures you to react to items as they arrive - regardless of their true priority.

I believe the more often you check email, the more often people will expect you to check it.

Checking your inbox for incoming email from time to time is not really a good habit especially if you are about to finish something or you are working towards the accomplishment of a goal.
Keep the checking to a minimum and allow yourself to focus on your work.

- Write and reply briefly. Be clear and to the point. Don't overcomplicate an explanation.

- Use "Text snippets" to deal with messages that require no follow up or where you plan to follow up on a later stage. Delete email immediately when no response is needed.

- Pick up the phone. Several minutes spent in replying to e-mail can be shortened tremendously by just calling the person. You'll get faster responses and you'll end up saving a lot of time. And of course, the personal touch is priceless.

- Do not use your email inbox as a place to manage your tasks, projects and communication.

- Terminate spam. Spam messages are very prevalent nowadays. Not only can they waste a lot of your time, but they can be very annoying as well. To prevent spam, don't spread your e-mail address around. If you can, make your e-mail address more intricate. For example, use marschall_jones27543@yahoo.com instead of marschall_jones@yahoo.com. If you're inserting your e-mail address into websites and messages, you may replace @ with "AT." For instance, write down marschall_jonesATyahoo.com instead of marschall_jones@yahoo.com.

- Get your e-mail across. Sometimes your e-mail could mistakenly be regarded as spam, and this would waste your time in composing that message. To prevent such occurrences, be careful with your choice of words. Avoid words or phrases that trigger the spam filters. Some words to avoid: free, money, sex, amazing, limited offer, naked, opportunity, debt, loans, lottery, retire, urgent.

14. Internet

Studies show that many of today's workers spend a lot of their time surfing the Internet. If you are one of these people, you are probably wasting time and costing your employer money. Many businesses are cracking down, and many Internet surfers are being shown the door.

How People Waste Their Time Surfing the Internet

The internet is extremely popular due to the many benefits that it offers, especially to those with online businesses. Nowadays, you will see people browsing the net frequently. Do you think that this is a good thing? Well, the internet has its advantages but it also presents some disadvantages as well.

Starting with its advantages, the internet is similar to a library where you can find almost anything that you need. It can help you get the information you need for a specific purpose. For instance, you need to conduct a research for a certain project in your school. All you have to do is to input your keyword and you will obtain many results for it. Whether you need information about entertainment, education or sports, you can get it through the internet. Furthermore, the internet also offers various services such as instant messengers and social networking sites that allow you to have communication with your friends or relatives. With these things, you can say that it offers numerous advantages. However, the internet also has another side to it.

The internet makes some people decadent. You can clearly see this in many students who utilize the internet to play various games and easily become addicted to it, which can lead them to neglect their school work. Many lack self-control. You can observe that there are lots of students who play games all day till night and totally forget about their school projects, work and assignments. In the end, their grades drop and they totally fail their subjects. What's worse is they will not be accepted in college due to their low grades. Although the problem may start as a simple one, its consequences should be well thought out to avoid even bigger problems in the future.

With this, you can say that they are just wasting their time surfing the net to play the games that they are addicted to. Getting addicted to the internet can also lead one to neglect his or her responsibilities. For instance, if one surfs the net all the time, he or she may forget that an important task is waiting to be done. This in turn could result in one getting fired from or having additional work. As you can figure, getting addicted to the internet is not a good thing as it can negatively affect one's life.

In general, the internet is a good thing as long as you know how to control yourself. You can find various forms of entertainment online but you should not be addicted to any of these things, as this can lead you to neglect many other significant things and persons in your life. Keep in mind that anything which is done more than normal is not good. With this, you should know when to use and when to stop using the internet to avoid wasting your time and suffer its negative effects on the quality of the life that you are living right now.

15. Phone calls

You don't have to answer every time it rings. To avoid wasting time with phone calls try the following:

- If you have blocked out a certain time for working on a task do not let phone calls interrupt your momentum. Turn off your phone for two hours while you complete your task. If that is too much, then do it for one hour or for thirty minutes. While you may feel that you need to be "on call" always, the truth is that you are losing productivity by allowing continual interruptions to your workflow.

- If you have a receptionist or an assistant, ask that your calls be held for the allotted time (making exceptions for urgent ones).

- If you must answer a phone call and the person can wait, ask them for a time when you can call back and discuss the issue. Not only will you set boundaries with your time but you can be prepared to deal with the call without other distractions.

Telephones require the use of your hand, which makes it difficult to do other tasks when you are talking. Invest in a headset if you can. It will free up both of your hands so you can do other things while you talk.

16. How to Deal with Interruptions and Remain Productive

When you are busily working at your computer, those pop-up announcements that you have a new e-mail in your inbox, or a message from your MSN or Yahoo messenger can take away from your productivity. Pop-up announcements do promote multi-tasking, but this is not something that you want to do when you have priority items that need to be completed by certain deadlines.

In the midst of work-related deadlines and other responsibilities, interruptions are unpredictable and bound to happen. At times it may appear to be harmless when it first starts, but as it continues to happen throughout the day it multiplies, causing you to become unfocused, overwhelmed, and even frustrated. The effect of interruptions can often be extreme stress.

Although we would like to believe that we can multi-task and be flexible to what the day brings, interruptions do compound and take away from productivity if you let it. It removes your focus on the task at hand, and into a different task and/or situation. It can cause your work to become unproductive, inefficient, and unmanageable. It can even effect your own satisfaction with your work.

Whether interruptions come in the form of an urgent meeting, unexpected personal demands, email, or time-wasting conversations with co-workers, it has a direct way of stealing our precious time. As this happens each day, it becomes more irritable for us and changes our moods to a negative state, especially when there is important work to be done.

Some interruptions can be avoided, but many can't. It is your responsibility to learn to decipher between what interruptions are necessary, and what ones are not. Learning to manage this better is an alternative to those interruptions that can't be avoided.

In dealing with messenger interruptions when working on your computer, make sure your current status reflects that you are busy or offline. This will eliminate you being distracted by unnecessary messages. If you place your current status as busy, you can add a message that will say you will respond at a later time, or any other personal message that is professional, yet cordial. This will notify the person that is trying to contact you that you currently can't be disturbed, but find their message important and will respond at a later time.

If you see that the matter is of a pressing nature, you then have the choice to take care of the situation at that moment, or finish a section of the task you are working on first. You may find that many requests, although they may seem urgent to the sender, can be postponed to a later time. This then gives you the power to determine when you will address the person's need. For example, you can schedule a meeting with this person, or place the task on your calendar for the next day. This is where prioritizing also plays an important role.

By choosing this approach, you keep your workload manageable without becoming stressed and feeling overwhelmed. You are still honoring the other person's request, but at the same time you are also honoring your time. There is no need to compete with interruptions. Learn to manage them effectively, while still respecting the other person's needs.

Whenever you begin to work on your prioritized tasks for the day, you never know what the day's distractions will bring. So there is a part of you that must remain flexible in your schedule. An important e-mail or phone call may be received, that needs to be addressed immediately. This is being flexible.

Don't let the feeling of expecting interruptions ruin your focus on your current task. This will not allow you to truly relax and focus on your important task. The reality is that, yes, interruptions do destroy your concentration, but remember that you have control over some and no control over other interruptions. Loss of concentration does equal the loss of your creative work, so it can be frustrating. What you don't want to do is end up in a "reactive mode". Prioritize and focus on what needs to be done and take interruptions based on importance.

17. Drop-In Visitors

You're busy working on a pressing work project that is approaching a deadline, and you suddenly hear, "Do you have a minute?" Has this questions always turned into longer than a minute after you politely said, "Yes?" This is very common and can rob you of your productive time.

Co-workers stopping by your office for that so-called 'one minute' of your time can end up depriving you of finishing your task on time. In fact, if your entire day is filled with this 'one minute' of your time requests, your productivity can decline drastically. Individuals that ask for a minute of your time can quickly become comfortable in the conversation with you and start discussing other issues not related to the original request of your time.

While there are companies that practice the 'open door' policy, or you may not be fortunate enough to have an office with a door that can be closed for privacy, it is essential to have time that is scheduled for un-interruption. This is the only way your prioritized tasks can be completed. To prevent the wasting of your precious time from unexpected 'drop-in' visitors, try using some of the following suggestions:

- Change the layout of your desk so you are not facing the people traffic outside of your office. Any eye contact can lead to uninvited interruptions.

- Move any items located in your office that need to be frequented by others, such as common files, to a general office area away from your work space.

- Each day, block time in your daily schedule for priorities and stick to it as much as possible. Tackle large, important projects or tasks early in the morning before reading e-mail or any interruptions can occur. Of equal importance, is setting quiet time for just you during the day. Avoid eating lunch at your desk, as people will assume you are always available.

- Communicate to fellow co-workers that you are not available at a certain period of time during the morning, and will only accept meetings after that time.

- Schedule time that you are not available, and stick to that schedule.

- If you have your own office, isolate yourself by closing your door. You may even consider putting a "do not disturb" sign on your door. If you don't have an office, see if you can work in a conference room in private.

- If you are able, consider using some work days to telecommute. You'll be surprised how much more you can get done at home during uninterrupted time that at work.

- Don't feel obligated that you have to have an open door policy. This only gives people the power to manage your time, taking away that power from you. The true meaning of an open door policy is that you are generally available for communication when your schedule permits. This policy does not mean that you are always available at someone's request.

- If you have an assistant, have he or she assist you with managing your time. Set up clear guidelines on when you are available to meet with others, and when you are not. Have your assistant schedule your meetings according to your work calendar.

- If there is no escaping dealing with an individual, especially if it is an urgent situation, gather the details of the situation and either handle immediately or schedule another time during the day for the meeting. Ensure you know have an idea of how much time this will take.

- If someone asks for a moment of your time or if you are free at the moment, ask them to schedule a time to meet with you later in the day.

- To avoid continuous interruptions from co-workers, politely ask them in advance to gather all the information that they need to talk to you about and schedule a time in the afternoon to review all items at once. This is a great time-saver and interruption minimizer.

- If people walk in your office and just want to "talk stories", politely tell them if they can sum up the situation as you have an important task you are working on.

- If you have chairs in your office, discourage people from sitting and having long conversations with you by placing items, such as your briefcase on the chairs. Empty chairs are very inviting to some.

If there are individuals that will not take the hint that a meeting has to be scheduled, or that you are busy working on a project, try using some of these tips. It may come across as being rude, but it is necessary for some people:

- Invent a meeting that you need to leave for.

- Inform the person that you have an important phone call to make regarding an urgent issue. This may bring the ongoing conversation to an end.

- Set a time limit for the conversation. Check the time in an obvious manner, and make sure to say that the time is up and you need to get back to your task.

Mark Woods, author of Attack Your Day! Before It Attacks You: Activities Rule Not the Clock, chooses to use interruptions with a color-coding system. This is used as a guide to deal with the four main types of interruptions that can exist in a work place. The interruptions are coded in red, green, yellow, and grey.

This color system assists you in dealing with continuous interruptions so you can spend more time in production. It's this simple – when an interruption enters, question yourself on what color this is associated to.

- Red – Urgent and important situation. This is something that needs to be handled immediately. This is where you need to stop working on your job and address the urgent situation right away.

- Green – The interruption may not be an emergency, but it is still something that must be acted on promptly and not postponed.

- Yellow – This is an interruption that does not require urgent attention. It is something that you need to deal with, but it can be scheduled for later in the day or the next day.

- Grey – These are the interruptions that are a complete waste of time. The only response this deserves is "no".

Ensure that your tactics are not counterproductive to the environment of your organization. You don't want your benefits to undermine the overall feeling of your work place and what may be common practice. Sometimes, isolating yourself is necessary; otherwise you will get no work done. It may frustrate others, but you have to respect your time and your deadlines. It is okay for them to waste their own time, but not yours.

18. Developing the Ability to Say "No"

In general, people find it difficult saying 'no' when being asked to do something, attend an event or party, or something as simple as visiting a friend. The most trying part of not being able to say no, is that you may be asked to do something you really don't want to do. You run the risk of being taken advantage of, not to mention the undue stress caused to yourself, because you really wanted to say no.

So why do we feel we need to say yes, when we really want to say no? Maybe it's the fear of not being liked, the need to make others happy, or the need to please. It is a feeling of guilt that is more overpowering than having enough respect for ourselves and to say no honestly with no regrets.

Understanding Your Right to Say "No"

When asked to do anything that you truly do not want to do or participate in, keep the following in mind:

- You have every right to say no.

- Don't let anyone take advantage of you. When you always say yes, you set yourself up as the person that everyone goes to when they need something done.

- Saying no is not rude. Use a calm voice, and politely say, "No."

- You do not need a reason or an excuse for saying no.

- When you already have plans or goals set for yourself, do not feel guilt in saying no. Have respect for your needs.

- Even when someone continues to pursue asking you for that favor after you have said no, stick with your answer.

Repeat it as many times as you have to, until the person understands that you really mean no.

Saying "No" to Your Boss

There is great fear in saying no to your boss; however, respect is a two-way street. When respect is given, respect is received. So what do you do if your boss asks you to complete a task that will turn your schedule upside down or even cause you to work late when you had after work plans? It's important to be flexible in the work place, but not by losing your respect. Here are some respectful ways of saying no, without really using the word 'no':

- Share your priority list with your boss. Explain to your boss the other priorities you have for the day, and ask where his or her task fits in with the work that was already given to you.

- Have your boss make the decision of what will be done and what will have to wait until tomorrow.

- If your boss insists that everything is a priority, explain that within the time frame given, your best work may not be done when divided amongst all those tasks.

- Provide an alternative to your boss, that the task he or she wants done can't be completed by you today, but you can work on it first thing in the morning. Or suggest that someone else in the office can provide support to your boss.

Most importantly, whether it's a friend, co-worker, parent, or boss that asks you to do something, saying no does not require any type of justification or reasoning. Keeping your response short will prove to the person asking you for something that you are honest, credible, and respectful.

Simple Ways to Say "No" Now

There may be times where you need to say no in the present, but you would like to keep your options open if you think you may change your mind. Here are four simple ways to nicely say no with the option to say yes later if you choose to:

- "That sounds like so much fun!"

- "That sounds like a great idea! You should begin pursuing that."

- "I would love to help you right now, but I can't. Maybe next time."

- "Wow, I'm flattered that you asked me, but this is not a good time for me at the moment."

- "I would love to help you, but maybe _____ can assist you?"

- "I'm unable to help you at this moment, have you considered _____?"

Saying "No" with Tact

Having self-respect means that you don't always have to say yes, and there may be times that no is the only option. Avoid pressuring yourself and allowing stress to take over your day by saying "no" with tact. It keeps your confidence up and allows others to have respect for you.

- Be firm. It is not necessary to be overly apologetic or defensive with your response. As long as you keep an even tone in your voice, and be polite, your response will be taken with respect.

- Don't build false hopes. If you mean no, stick to it. Don't give the person asking any options that you may change your mind.

- Don't promise to get back to the person if your intention will still be to say no. Building a false promise can decrease your credibility.

- If you are unsure if you can say assist or attend a function, say, no. It is easier to say no from the beginning then saying "yes" and having to rescind your agreement.

- If you are asked for an explanation when you say no, remember that this is not something that you have to do. Stick with no.

When Saying "Yes" is Unavoidable

Then there are times that you cannot say no. Saying yes may be the only wise choice in a particular situation. Here are some examples of when saying yes is unavoidable:

- Inform the person asking you for help or to do something, that you will help him or her this time, but in the future you would prefer more notice so you can plan your day.

- Let the person know that he or she now owes you one, when you agree to help him or her with a situation. There is no shame in that. This is showing that you respect yourself.

- Provide the person doing the asking that you will get back to him or her with a timeframe of when that task can be completed, after you check your schedule.

- Be honest about how much time you have left in your day and that is all that you can offer in assistance. This way you are helping, but still respecting your time as well.

Saying no can be the most difficult thing you may have to do. It is difficult for many people, especially those with a low self-esteem. When you have a low self-esteem, you often lack the assertiveness needed to say no. This in turn makes you feel that you have to meet everyone's expectations or you won't be accepted.

It is hard to set boundaries with others. To avoid this feeling of being ashamed, guilty, or fearful, we are often quick to say yes without thinking the situation through until later when the stress and unhappiness sets in. You may begin to feel used and resentful of the person.

You always have the right to say no when saying yes is not beneficial to you. Learning to actually say no is not easy, but it can be one of the best things you can do for yourself. It can also be the best thing to do for the ones around you that you love. Your stress level will be low, and you can actually enjoy the things you really wanted to do.

If dealing with pushy people that will keep asking you for something even after you have said no causes you more guilt, continue to remain firm in your answer. If you are unable to stand firm at that time, then simply say you need to think about the request and get back to them. This will give you time to think and build your courage to stand up for yourself in respect. It's a tactic that will diminish the feeling of being pressured into doing something that you do not want to do.

Saying no is perfectly acceptable. You should always consider the time you are already committed to in regards to your career and personal life when you are asked to do something or attend something for someone else. No matter the situation, realize that your time is valuable and there is only so much that you can do in a day. Take a look at what you will be giving up if you make commitments to others that you really did not want to commit to.

Some main points that you should remember about saying "no" are:

- You are standing up for yourself as a person by stating how you feel.

- You are the sole proprietor of your time and your life.

- Saying no is not a sign of your weakness. It is a sign of your strength.

- Know your abilities and limitations when taking on more.

- You always deserve to have time to yourself and not take on more than you can handle physically or emotionally.

- Feel good in your honesty and respect for yourself.

Remind yourself of these things on a regular basis. Always know that it is okay to say no when you have to. No one is living your life and taking care of your responsibilities, so don't feel pressured of having to please anyone else. Please yourself first; it will make you a better person to others.

19. Conducting Productive Meetings

Did you ever come out of a meeting feeling that nothing was accomplished and it was a waste of your time? If a meeting is causing you to feel and think this way, most often it is because of poor planning. Unproductive meetings can also take time away from actually getting important work done. This generalization of meetings may be more common than many of us would like to believe.

On the other hand, meetings are not always unproductive. It is necessary for conducting an effective business, sporting event, or running a non-profit organization when there are many people on the team of which input is needed. In order to keep everyone informed about the organization or business' happenings, meetings are an essential means of communication.

When meetings are conducted, valuable information can be shared such as group issues, planning, and constructive feedback on operations or events. It is when meetings are called at the last minute, with no set agenda, plan, or directive, that people become upset. Also, if items can be dealt with one-on-one or through email, avoid setting a meeting. Generally, this is seen as another waste of time.

To avoid ineffective meetings, with no results and no action, the following guidelines might be helpful:

- Meetings are meant for people to come together for a common purpose to discuss items that can't be done with a few team members. Meetings are meant to inform and receive information from all key players. Proper planning and effective facilitation can lead to people feeling that their time was not wasted.

- Schedule meetings ahead of time, giving participants adequate time to plan their schedules. Some of the best times are later in the day or first thing in the morning. What is important is adequate meeting notice.

- An agenda should always be created, including the topic for discussion and who will be facilitating that topic. High priority topics should always be discussed first, in the event that you run out of time towards the end of the meeting.

- The agenda should be sent well in advance of the meeting. This gives the participants time to prepare for the topics that will be discussed.

- Have the time and place listed on the agenda, and begin the meeting promptly. This will soon teach participants that time is taken seriously at meetings and tardiness will not be tolerated.

- Inform all participants that cell phones and other technical devices are not to be used during the meeting for any other purpose than taking notes. Cell phones should always be turned off.

- Each agenda topic should have time for discussion, and a set time for outcomes. If no clear outcome can be reached, a set time for follow-up should be established for the next scheduled meeting. Assignments of follow-up items should also be delegated at this time.

- The meeting should be held at the time it was scheduled for. Any items not discussed by the end of the meeting should be placed first on the next meeting's schedule.

- At the end of the meeting, the meeting facilitator or note taker should review follow-up actions so everyone is clear on his or her responsibilities.

20. Delegate

When you decide to delegate, you decide to give something to someone else. It can be power, responsibility, or an assignment. The practice of delegation can be an effective way of saving you time to perform other tasks or activities, allowing for a better balance of your life.

And for all you know, the other person may do a better job than you! Or the other person may come up with an easier way of doing something that you never even considered.

There are many excuses for choosing not to delegate. Some of the most commonly used reasons included:

- "I can do it better if I do it myself."

- "If I want it done correctly the first time, I rather do it myself."

- "No one is as capable or knowledgeable as me; I need to do it myself."

- "It is a waste of my time to train someone on doing the task."

- "There is no one qualified enough for me to delegate this task to."

- "Everyone already has enough to do."

- "I am the only one who knows how to do this."

What if you assumed that some people would love to have added responsibilities? Don't you sometimes feel honored when someone puts you in charge of a certain project? Doesn't it feel empowering when your boss entrusts you with a very important task? Make the assumption that people want to learn; that they want more

71

responsibility to foster personal growth. On the other hand, your little investment of time in training others means more time for you to tackle other tasks or enjoy free time with your family.

Delegation is most commonly found in the business environment. Approaching someone in a positive manner to assist you with a task, even if you are not the boss, can empower others and help you. It is all in how you approach people to help you. Have the right approach with the right tone of voice, and you can get anyone to assist you. Take the wrong approach, and forget about receiving help. This practice can also be done with household tasks.

Determining What to Delegate

Only delegate what you would do yourself. If you wouldn't do the task or activity, don't delegate it to someone else. There is more respect, when the other person knows it is something that you have done in the past, or would do. There are several examples of things that you can delegate both in the work environment and in the household:

- Research assignments

- Fact-finding assignments

- Preparing rough drafts of standard correspondence

- Preparing rough drafts of routine reports

- Photocopying

- Data entry

- House cleaning

- Washing clothes

- Watching young children

- Washing the car

The lists are endless. In the work environment, it is also helpful to cross-train other employees so that in your absence, the work can continue. It is not only beneficial to you, by not coming back to work with a mountain of assignments, but it is also beneficial to the employer. The work can continue regardless of who is out sick or on vacation.

Some business tasks that are commonly used in cross-training include: payroll, mail deliveries, software assistance, answering phones, accounting, and travel arrangements.

Remember, when you delegate a task, ensure that the directions for completion are clear. Investing time in clear communication can decrease the chance of the task being done incorrectly and having to be redone.

Delegation of a task does not take away of your responsibility. Someone else may be assisting you, but it will still be your responsibility to ensure that the task is completed correctly and on time. It's a learning process for all. It's a new learning experience for one person, and it's a managing experience for another.

How to Delegate

Now that you know things can be delegated, how do you actually delegate?

- Delegate to different people. Avoid delegating to the same person all the time. Give others a chance.

- Give different people experience that they may want to expand their career options or personal growth.

- Have clear communication on the expectations of the delegated task. This includes what needs to be done and when it needs to be completed by.

- Ensure that you give the person authority over the delegated project or task. This allows the person to feel a personal attachment to completing the task accurately.

- Have trust in the person you delegate the work to. Don't hover over him or her, checking every detail. Let the person take charge of the task.

- Set small check points for the person you delegated the task to. This will not only give you reassurance that the job is being done correctly, but this is an opportunity for you to give positive feedback.

- Check-in with the person that you delegated the task to. See how things are going, but don't check-in to micromanage.

- There may be some errors that occur along the way. Be accepting of this as a learning experience.

- After giving clear instructions on the task at hand, always ask the person if he or she needs anything to make the job easier.

- Once the task has been completed, always give appreciation.

Assignment

Create a list of tasks that you can delegate to someone else. Under each task, list the following:

- Goal(s)

- Who assigned to?

- Is asking for assistance realistic?

- Deadline for completion of task.

Take these tasks and begin the delegation. The need to delegate is always ongoing, as there are always things that need to be done, whether in the business world or at home. Delegating can be a great way to save time by being able to complete other tasks or enjoy other activities. This is a win-win situation for all.

21. Outsourcing

It's just like they say, no one is really perfect. We have our own flaws, our own faults and our own weaknesses. We cannot excel in all aspects of life. Sometimes we do poorly on some things and do not know how to finish other chores successfully.

Life is not perfect and neither are we.

Why am I stating the obvious? Well, it is because in our private lives and working lives we are bound to do things that, if we do not hate them, just do not have a clue how to finish or sometimes even start them in the right way. We lack the skill, the inspiration, the knowledge; in short, we do poorly on the assigned task.

Just face it, and never be too shy to admit that sometimes we aren't the best person for a certain job, while others might well be better.

If you feel like things are not going your way, or that the job you have is something you actually hate, or you are just not good at it, always remember that it is never bad to ask for help.

You can always reach out and ask someone else to do it for you or help you with it. Yet, when doing this, always keep in mind that good things do not always come for free.

Stephen Covey's image describing the Emotional Bank Account (from his book The Seven Habits of Highly Effective People) certainly is one of the most formidable ideas ever put forward on the development of relationships between people.

In essence it means that anyone with whom we have a relationship, regardless of whether it is our coworker, friend or family, we keep up a personal 'emotional' bank account with them. This account always starts with a clean slate. And just as with any other bank account, we can make deposits and withdrawals.

However, instead of dealing with units of monetary value, we deal with emotional units. Stephen Covey mentions six major ways of making deposits in the Emotional Bank Account: attending to little things, understanding the person, clarifying expectations, keeping commitments, showing personal integrity, and apologizing sincerely when you make a 'withdrawal'.

When you are caring, kind, honest, and friendly to another person, you make deposits in their Emotional Bank Account. However, if you are disrespectful, unkind, mean and uncaring, you draw from this account. Always keep this in mind when you ask for help or are asked for help as a favor.

If you are able and willing to pay, you know that hiring someone else to do your work comes with an added monetary cost.

If you have the money to hire do not be afraid to hire someone else. These costs might eventually help you boost your business or help you yield greater income, or it might help you free time to do some fun stuff with the family or read a book. Just make sure that the one you are hiring really does have knowledge of the job you assign to him or her. Check credentials before giving him/her the job and letting him/her be on board.

Yet, if you are on a tight budget and you feel like you cannot afford to have another one do it for you and get paid, there is always a thing called 'trading'.

You can always work together and help each other. You can trade skills and share your knowledge.
Let's say for example, you are good in putting up blogs and making websites yet you are poor in creating content for your blog. You can always work with someone who knows how to write and in exchange teach that person how to put up blogs and design websites.

In this way, both of you are learning and helping each other to excel in the field that both of you are poor at, and at the same time in the field that both of you are good at.

You will be making deposits and withdrawals from the emotional bank account between you both.
Being able to help each other is a good thing! In fact, helping each other can yield greater and much better results than you might have anticipated beforehand.

So, when you are in need, tap someone on the shoulder and ask for help, and at the same time, help the other person too.

22. A Supportive and Effective Mindset

23. Stay Motivated

Motivation is the perseverance in times of distress. It is what keeps us from quitting just before we reach the finish line. Yes, we often quit when we are just about to obtain our goals. So why would anyone want to do that? Why does that happen? The reason is that we never know how close we are to that finish line.

Motivation is a powerful component that can drive you past the finish line into completion of your goals. Everyone has different factors that provide motivation. Some motivational skills come into play naturally, while some are developed by influential outside factors.

In order to activate your motivation through the setbacks and obstacles that life delivers, you must remain focused on the end result. Focusing on the feeling that will engulf your body and spirit when you achieve your goal is the success obtained through sheer motivation. This is the secret of all great achievers. They never give up. They find what motivates them, and they keep pushing through until they obtain their goals. They continue to persist until success is achieved.

You can achieve this success too by finding that burning desire that causes intense motivation to trigger. Motivation comes from deep within you. It comes from a sense of purpose. It's a type of purpose that is developed when you have made the decision to stand up for what is right for you, and you alone. It is based on what you value as a person and what will bring you great happiness. Your goals must always be based on these principles. This is the most important step in setting and achieving goals.

Some may say that just setting specific and attainable goals is motivation enough to move you towards goal achievement; however, the reality is that the circumstances surrounding the achievement of a goal can be difficult and cause discomfort. This discomfort and pain involved in reaching your goals can kill your motivation, because you lose focus on the big picture.

No matter what your goals are, from getting in great physical health, to saving for a large purchase or vacation, or obtaining that rewarding career, motivation is the secret to keep you on track until success is reached. Here are some tips that can assist you in remaining motivated no matter what curves life may throw at you.

Think of the end result.

Take your goal, write it down with clarity, ensure that you can measure your steps towards your goal, make sure it is attainable for you, and add a timeline. The timeline doesn't have to be of a completion date, but can be small attainable steps to your goal.

The next step is to really 'feel' your goal. Imagine what it will look like and how you will feel. Envision yourself achieving your goal. This will help you stay motivated.

Composing a dream board of pictures replicating your goal at completion can be an excellent daily motivator. For example, if you want to save money for your dream vacation, but you have a habit of spending money on needless items, collect travel brochures and pictures of your travel destination to add to your 'dream board'. Looking at this dream board each day will keep your mind focused on what is important for the future, and not be distracted by the present.

Reward yourself for small victories.

It is natural to want something, and to want it now. We live in a fast-paced world, so how could we expect any different? In reality, goals with deeper meanings may require some effort on your part to achieve success. You can't let this deter you from losing focus on the end result.

If you are easily distracted or get bored with the tedious steps required to reach your goal, you may find that awarding yourself for each step you take towards your main goal can lead to big results. The small rewards are little incentives to keep you motivated. Even something such as a special flavored coffee treat can be a nice motivation and build your self-confidence, pushing you through to your final goal. Keep the rewards reasonable; it doesn't have to be extravagant. However, you want to ensure that it is done frequently to keep you on the right momentum to success.

Draw inspiration from others.

There are many avenues to seek out inspiration for keeping yourself motivated. Some of these inspirational sources can come from quotes, music lyrics, movies, or even from ordinary people you know who have achieved goals similar to your own.

You may even consider working with someone in partnership. This person may provide the motivational support you need to keep you accountable to your goal. Even a life partner can be a great inspiration in encouraging you to stick with the small steps to goal achievement. There is great magic to be found in friends who are achieving their goals, are happy, and serve as a great inspiration towards your success.

Even speaking to successful people, motivational speakers, mentors, and life coaches can inspire you tremendously.

Give yourself more autonomy.

When you develop a goal you need to take ownership over it. Dictate how you will accomplish that goal. Decide when you will work on your goal. Be creative in your ownership and truly make the goal your own.

Increase your sense of mastery.

On your path to achieving your goal you will learn many new things along the way about yourself and about the goal itself. Your skills and your capabilities will increase as a direct result of your work on achieving your goal. Be passionate about what you are doing. Each day push yourself a little further in the process to success.

Enjoy the feeling of accomplishment.

Have confidence in your work and in the steps you are taking to succeed. Each day you complete a task that takes you closer to your goal; there will be a feeling of accomplishment and confidence. Understandably, it may be very difficult in the beginning, but keep pursuing. The incredible feeling that you will experience at the end will be an overwhelming feeling of accomplishment.

More motivational tips:

1. Visualization
   Think of a goal that you want to accomplish. Think in detail of your end result once you complete your goal. Picture yourself achieving and reaching your goal activating all of your senses.

2. Music and Movies
   Get a notebook or piece of paper and make a list of CDs and DVDs that inspire you. Purchase the music CD that makes you feel good when you hear it on the radio. You can even purchase an inspirational movie that instantly makes you feel motivated deep within. Listen to the CDs and watch the DVDs every time you need to boost your morale. All these simple things can be used when you are down and need that extra boost of motivation.

3. Collect Inspirational Quotes
   Collect motivational quotes and place them all around you. Post success and inspirational quotes to your computer, on your mirror, or on your nightstand. You can log it in a

notebook and review it first thing in the morning, at night, or any time you need a motivational boost.
Some positive affirmations include:

- a. "I am strong and healthy and I am in full control of my life."
- b. "I am in full control of achieving anything I want in my life."
- c. "I am full of positive energy and vitality to accomplish all tasks set before me."

4. Use Success Creeds
   A success creed is a statement that is used to define the value that is of importance to you, and which you intend to stick to during your pursuit of success. Some examples of success creeds are:

   - a. "I will give one hundred percent of my efforts and thoughts to everything that I do."
   - b. "I will treat everyone that I come in contact with in a manner that is respectful, and I will treat myself with the same respect."
   - c. "I will make the right choice in everything that I do and say."
   - d. "I will direct my energies towards prosperity and success by remaining focused on the end result that I have designed for myself."

5. Use Success Questions
   Success questions are used to maintain your focus on the many internal thoughts that travel in your mind. By regularly reviewing your success questions you will remain focused and lessen any external negative influences that turn into negative thoughts. Some examples of success questions are:

   - a. "What type of exercise can I do today to step closer to my goal?"
   - b. "What can I do right now to assist me in obtaining my goal of _____?"
   - c. "What can I physically do today to bring me closer to achieving my goal of _____?"

6. Regain Control over Internal Thoughts
   Focus your thoughts on the positive end results and the positive steps that you have taken and are taking to achieve success of accomplishing your goal. Remove negative thoughts from your mind by replacing them with positive thoughts. Use what you need to keep you positive, such as the following:
   a. "I know that as one door closes, another door opens."
   b. "I will always do things with good intentions."
   c. "I understand that it takes work to achieve a goal and I accept that."
   d. "I am in charge of my own life."
   e. "I am open, receptive, and obedient to what life delivers to me on my path to success."

No matter how you choose to use these motivational tools, they can help in keeping you focused. Choose what works for you. These are just guidelines that can be mixed with your own creativity. Do what makes you happy and keeps you focused on the ultimate reward – your goal.

24. Stay Focused

It's very important to attain focus when you work on chores that need you to pay full attention. Details often do matter; think of writing a sales letter, bookkeeping, coding software, Photoshop design or wire-framing, to name just a few.

You can keep your focus by making a commitment to yourself to work on a certain chore for a period of time before moving to something else. You use a schedule!

You can keep a timer to guard the time frame you allocated to do the job.

Another prerequisite to focus is to avoid all distractions; distractions in your environment (noise, sounds, movement, heat etcetera), and clutter or distractions running through your head.

If you experience thoughts that distract you, briefly jot them down and continue with the job at hand. If you are working at a computer be sure to turn off your internet or at least social media like Twitter, Facebook, Pinterest or Google. You will soon realize you'll be delivering better quality on your job in less time.

25. Focus on Your Strengths

Another commonality among people who successfully manage their time is focusing on their strong traits. How often do well-intentioned friends, colleagues, managers and others tell you to labor on your shortcomings? Often, trying to work on your weak spots might be the worst action you can take!

Now I'm not speaking about picking up certain knowledge or skills you lack at the moment. It is paramount that you get that knowledge or skill if you need it to reach an important goal. But what if you prove consistently to be "lousy" at something, or find it hard to master, regardless of how much effort you put into it – like learning a foreign language, or understanding math? Someone musically inept should probably not strive to be the next James Taylor.

Good news: You can't excel at everything and quite certainly you never will. So you can quit wasting time trying. You are unique, with your own specific set of talents and abilities. You have character strengths; are you upbeat, optimistic, kind, devoted, determined?

You also have ability strengths (natural abilities); are you a strong competitor, creative, innovative, a logistical thinker, a problem solver, a singer, an athlete, a musician?

You have talents (learned abilities); are you a gardener, a pilot, a writer, a chef, a computer programmer, a craftsman, an artist? Enjoy yourself for who you are.

So will you nonetheless go on squandering your valuable time bending over backwards to get a little bit better at that one thing that just doesn't, and probably never will, come naturally – or do you plan to develop your true talents?

Truth is, you'll achieve far more value, regardless how you calculate that term (income, outcomes, accomplishments, or another measurement), not to mention happiness, by focusing and improving on your strengths.

Assignment

Go to a place where you will not be disturbed. Take some time to focus on your strengths. List your character strengths, ability strengths, and talents. List as many as you can think of – don't be humble, don't be modest. Celebrate the uniqueness of you. Which of these strengths will benefit you as you move toward achievement of your goals? Struggling to excel at traits that are just not you is a waste of time. Forget about them. Instead, work to excel at your strengths.

26. Don't Procrastinate

Procrastination is experienced by everyone on occasion at different levels. Some people may be chronic procrastinators, while others enjoy working under the pressure of multiple projects and deadlines. Procrastination has nothing to do with being a lazy person. It can be associated with just running out of time to complete assignments or tasks, or just a matter of taking on too many responsibilities.

Lots of the things that we end up procrastinating about, we usually identify with being boring, difficult, overwhelming, or complicated. A high percentage of people procrastinate, because they simply feel overwhelmed. When you feel overwhelmed, it's almost like a defense mechanism being triggered, and you may begin to procrastinate and deadlines become harder to meet.

Procrastination means the habit of putting off what you can do now to a later date. When you procrastinate, you are putting off the completion of a task, project, or responsibility that has some benefit to you, however, for an unexplained reason you have more energy to put off what needs to be done than actually doing what needs to be done. Studies have shown that 9 out of 10 people practice procrastination. Procrastination is practiced more often than we think.

Five Negative Effects of Procrastination

1. Morale is broken down as you feel the effects of a job left uncompleted.

2. Efficiency is diminished by the clutter left from unfinished jobs.

3. Stress levels can increase as jobs that are procrastinated can start to accumulate and become due at the same time.

4. Others can view you as lazy and having a lack of interest in the job at hand.

5. As jobs are postponed, it becomes more unpleasant to complete.

Causes and Remedies for Procrastination

- Cause: You may be having trouble getting started.
  Remedy: Start small. Complete one small part of the task at hand to get your energy flowing. Once you begin the flow will continue on completing more and more of the task. Getting started is the hardest part, but once you do the road to completion will become easier.
  Example: If your goal is to lose weight and begin an exercise program, start with doing just 10 minutes three times per week. Slowly increase this time until you are doing 20-30 minutes three times per week. Starting out slow will give you the determination to stick to the plan.

- Cause: You may view the task as being too complex and you become unable to get started on the task, followed with a feeling of being overwhelmed.
  Remedy: Take the task and separate it into smaller parts that are manageable for you throughout today and the following days. Some people work better when a large task is divided into smaller sections allowing for a great feeling of completion, which will move them on the road to goal accomplishment.
  Example: When given a large project to complete at work, review the entire project then ask yourself this question first – "What is the easiest means for me to get started on this project?" Once you've identified this – JUST DO IT!

- Cause: Feeling of Failure to Achieve Goal
  Remedy: Break a goal down into short-term goals that are achievable by realistic deadlines.

- Cause: Distraction

  Remedy: Write down the task that needs to be completed. You can use something like a "to do" list, or use a weekly and/or monthly planning calendar. Put the steps of the task in priority order. This will give you a feeling of organization and a distinctive process to follow in completing the task.

- Cause: Lack of Time

  Remedy: This is a popular excuse, but being busy does not necessarily mean you are being productive. If you feel you are lacking time, it is most likely due to lack of organization, prioritizing, or the ability to say 'no' to taking on more tasks. Be responsible for your time to become more efficient. You'll be surprised at how many hours you actually do have in a day.

- Cause: Being too Hard on Yourself

  Remedy: Don't hold procrastination against yourself. Forgive yourself and move on planning out what tasks need to be done in a day.

- Cause: Unable to Prioritize

  Remedy: Schedule work to be done and specific times and do it. Stick to your schedule, whether you like it or not, because you will like the results in the end.

- Cause: Low Value Placed on Tasks

  Remedy: Relate a task to something that is attractive to you. Give yourself rewards for completing certain steps towards the task, and issuing punishment for any procrastination.

- Cause: Not Being Accountable for Taking Action

  Remedy: You may tend to slack in the completion of a task, especially if you are only responsible to yourself and not someone else. Try asking someone for assistance in monitoring your progress and holding you accountable.

- Cause: Thinking you have to be a Perfectionist
  Remedy: Always remember that nothing is always perfect,
  and sometimes it doesn't have to be. It just has to be the
  best that you have to offer. Accept your fears and anxieties
  about the task at hand, but don't let it get in the way of your
  accomplishments. It is never 'all or nothing'.

- Cause: Fear of Failure or Success
  Remedy: Fear of the final outcome of the task can be
  debilitating. You may have a fear of not being able to do
  the task perfectly or not meet the standards of completion,
  which can delay your progress. Some may fear the success.
  Success may lead to other options that maybe you don't
  think you are ready for. To avoid this fear, define clearly
  the consequences of completing or not completing the task
  you are responsible for.

- Cause: Hating the Task.
  This usually happens if you identify the task as boring,
  monotonous, or involving too much hard work.
  Remedy: Break the task down into smaller, manageable
  sections and give yourself one small task to work on at a
  time. Remember, rewards are always great, especially for
  challenging tasks that you really don't want to complete.

- Cause: Fear of Change
  Remedy: Change is hard, but it is essential to progress.
  Accept that change is hard, but tell yourself to be flexible
  and excited about change. Once you accept how you feel,
  and know that it is just a process you have to go through,
  procrastination can diminish.

Lies and Myths about Procrastination

A shared myth about procrastination is telling us that there is a
valid reason for putting off working on and completing a specific

task. The reality is that this is just an excuse, because we don't want to put the effort into concentrating on working on the task. There are four most commonly identifiable procrastination myths:

Myth 1: "I work better under pressure."
    The reality is that procrastination directly affects performance. When you try to complete tasks at the last minute, such as cramming for a big test by studying late into the night the day before the test, is not being efficient. Planning out your tasks, which allows you to pace yourself, is more efficient than waiting to the last possible moment to complete a task.

Myth 2: "I need to be inspired or in the right mood."
    This is procrastination in disguise. You need to just get to work, without waiting and waiting for ideas of inspiration to manifest in your mind. Inspiration occurs when you are disciplining yourself to do what you need to do to complete the task. When you do, you will be inspired.

Myth 3: "I need uninterrupted time to work on this task."

Myth 4: "I'll be able to do a much better job on this assignment tomorrow."

Procrastination can be a way of lying to yourself and removing yourself from reality. This is the reality:

- If you do not start taking steps to become more effective and productive today, it will be worse tomorrow as you crunch for time.

- If you do not take small steps to discipline yourself today, you will not be disciplined tomorrow.

- If you do not become organized today, the disorganization will only become worse tomorrow.

Ways to Beat Procrastination

There may be times when procrastination can be very hard to overcome. Here is a process you can use to accomplish those tasks:

- Make a list of all the tasks that you need to do, but have been putting off.

- Next to each item, write down your excuses for not completing it. Maybe it's a financial issue, or you don't think you are qualified, whatever the reason, write it down.

- Next to the excuses, write down the benefits that you presently enjoy, due to the fact that you are practicing procrastination on important tasks. There are benefits, because otherwise the tasks would be completed already.

- Look at your excuses and benefits for each item that you have procrastinated about. Does it really make sense? Are these excuses being emphasized by benefits? Are the benefits really that important and enough to make you stick to your excuses?

An item on your list may look like this:

Task (Compare excuses with benefits)
Item – Learn Spanish
Excuse – Do not have enough education
Benefit – Have more money if not spending on education and more time to do other things that I want to do instead of being in school.

Assignment

- Look over your list. Keeping the excuses and benefits in mind, decide which of the tasks you really want to do or need to do to reach accomplishment of the task. Highlight those tasks.

- Once you have accepted these things, and realize that it is okay for you to say that you don't really want that goal, give it up. If it is not important to you, there is no need to waste your time on something that you have a choice about.

Procrastination is not harmless. It has the power to destroy careers, marriages, and businesses. Change your attitude and habits of doing things later, to doing things now. It will make you feel better in the long term. If you really can't fight the procrastination on one task, complete another task and come back later to the task you procrastinated about. Accomplishing things gives you more confidence and determination to be productive.

27. Stop Multi-Tasking

Multi-tasking refers to carrying out multiple tasks somewhat simultaneously. The term comes from computer engineering. Multi-tasking is not an efficient way of completing tasks even though it seems you are achieving more in a particular period of time. This is because your brain is unable to focus simultaneously and hold the focus for one task while you are carrying out the other. What will happen is that your brain has to restart then focus on the task that you are doing and when you change to perform the other task, your brain will have to restart again and focus on the new task.

When this restart and focus function has to be done over and over again over a limited period of time, the brain will find it harder to process and refocus thus it has to drop some focus to manage, or it takes a longer period of time to be able to do the same thing as effectively. The more complex a task, the longer the time you will take to complete these complex tasks. It also takes longer to complete tasks that are different when multitasking. If the tasks you are juggling are totally different you will take a longer time or when doing tasks that you are unfamiliar with. This is because your brain needs a longer time to catch up and get focused on the task.

Because of the fragmented focus, productivity will dip as you will take a long time to complete the two or more tasks that you are juggling. The other problem with multi-tasking in relation to productivity is that you will not do your best work. This is because you are not absorbed in what you are doing long enough to get all the salient facts so you may get the general work done but you are likely to miss the finer details. These may get lost since your attention is just on the bigger picture.

This is best exemplified in the driving and using your cell phone scenario. If you are driving and you are on a phone call, you will be able to keep steering the car and keep moving, but in a situation that needs your quick reflexes or for you to make a judgment call such as swerving to avoid an oncoming car, your brain will take longer to make that call leading which may result in an accident.

If you want to get more work done efficiently in good time, the first thing is to stop multi-tasking. It may not be as easy as it seems, especially in a world where there is so much happening with the media, internet and other stimuli so that your brain is always receiving a lot of information. You have to learn to filter out what is not important to you at one given time. If for example you get into the office and you need to return three phone calls, check your email and meet a colleague or a client, you will need to decide which of these things is the most important.

Assign your tasks priority and a time limit. So if you have to go through three hundred emails, do it in an hour. What is not done in an hour you can designate to someone else or do it when you have ample time. If you find you are doing too much, or your responsibilities cannot be effectively done in the time limit you have assigned to them, then you may have to either delegate or step back from responsibilities.

Have a plan so that you can get everything done. Even if you do not do everything in one go, ensure that everything that needs to be done – gets done. This means you may have to plan and write down everything that needs to get done so that you do not forget. Be flexible so that you can change up your plan as need be, but only if it increases your time management or effectiveness. You need discipline so that even the work that is unappealing to you gets done in the time limit you have set for it. It is also easier to do similar tasks together so that you can save time.

28. Communication

Being a great communicator is necessary in making the best use of your time whilst being respectful of others people's time. Effective communication is listening attentively when the other person is talking and clearly explaining your thoughts when it is your turn to speak. Clearly understanding the needs of each other through focused listening is important for effective communication.

Many times, communication is based on a person's interpretation through unclear communication or inattentive listening. There are assumptions that are made, opinions that are developed, and ideas that are created that may not be factual. Effective communication creates a clear understanding of what is being said. Not understanding what is communicated is a waste of time for both parties involved in a discussion.

So how do you know that you are communicating your thoughts and ideas clearly to another person? How do you know that the person understands what you are communicating? You could just wait and see how your words are interpreted, or you could propose relevant questions to the person you are communicating with to ensure there is a clear understanding.

The Power of Thoughts and Words

There is great power in our words. Words can hurt and words can help. Words can be kind and words can be mean. There are a few common word phrases that we use that can be related to effective communication:

- "Yes, but..."
  This has two meanings. The first word is an agreement, and the second word means there's another opinion coming that could be positive or negative. It sets the tone that an opinion is going to be expressed. These words are often referred to as communication blockers. Listen when you speak, do you often use these two words?

- "Yes, and ... "
  These two words are a better option in communicating. It still allows you to express your opinion, but it has a much calmer and positive connotation. These two words have the power to improve the energy surrounding the discussion. It acknowledges and validates the opinion of the other person and his or her point of view. It also keeps a nice flow of communication between the two parties. These simple two words can make the difference in engaging in negative disagreements that go nowhere, and positive effective communication with direction and purpose.

- "Got to...", "Have to...", and "Must..."
  These words can be both empowering and disempowering. These words usually set the tone that there is no choice for the other person. Be careful of the words you choose.

- "Should"
  Be aware of what this word can mean when communicating. This would have been known to exemplify some form of guilt. For example, you say, "I should go exercise otherwise I will gain weight." The way you use the word "should" means that you will have a negative feeling, such as feeling bad for not doing something.

- "Never", "Forever", and "Always"
  These words have very definite generalizations about something, which may not even be true. Statements that use these words give the perception of directness in a negative sense. These words don't necessarily reflect the reality of the situation or discussion. These words are not clear and are not part of effective communication.

- "Try"
  This is a commonly used word, with an interesting meaning. Have you ever heard someone say, "Can you try and pick that up for me?" You cannot try to do something.

You either do it or you don't. Another example is asking someone to do something for you, and he or she replies with the word 'try'. You can gracefully assume that your request will not get done.

The Feedback Sandwich

Feedback is important in ensuring that your message has been communicated clearly. Feedback can be given and received to ensure effective understanding of the spoken message. It is essential to have an open mind and accept the feedback, whether it is positive or negative, for the focus can remain on clear communication; it shouldn't be taken personally.

Giving and receiving feedback can be difficult, but it is beneficial and effective – it is what makes up the 'feedback sandwich'. A feedback sandwich refers to the possibility of feedback containing criticism surrounded by praise. This type of feedback allows both the speaker and listener to view what may be perceived as the negatives in a constructive manner.

It means that you should begin your response to what is communicated with a positive statement, state what you don't understand, what may need more clarification, or what may need to be improved, followed by another positive statement. This is the full feedback sandwich approach for effective communication.

Here are some helpful tips to remember when practicing effective communication:

- Positive or negative feedback should always be directed only towards what is said without any words that could be interpreted as being attacking.

- Feedback should never be personal.

- Avoid direct feedback towards a person based on his or her character.

- Feedback should be constructive and focused on the discussion.

When offering positive statements of feedback, they should be focused on the desired behavior of the person and what is being discussed. At no time do you want to divert the focus from what is being discussed to something, for example, that is directed towards boosting one's ego. The recipient of the feedback should walk away from the conversation more informed about what was being discussed, rather than walking away with just a good feeling that has no purpose to what is being communicated. Both the praise and criticism of what is being discussed can begin with statements such as: "I really liked it when you said _____."; "When you said _____, I noticed that you_____."; and "I thought you use of _____ was really _____."

As part of the feedback of criticism, it should always be clear to what is being discussed. It must be objective and use "I" statements, rather than "you" statements. When saying "you" it becomes personal and can be taken as a personal attack, instead of constructive criticism. When giving this type of feedback, it is always a good idea to have realistic suggestions and alternatives to what is being discussed, if necessary.

Constructive criticism is much more than just being nice. It is a way to remain focused on the topic of discussion, and the person. Always be clear about the feedback in its pertinence to the discussion. Avoid vague statement that may leave the other person with more questions or confusion. It should always be said at the relevant time of the conversation after attentive listening has been completed. The criticism should remain specific and be within the person's control. Always avoid words such as, 'always' and 'never', which starts to become too personal.

Giving constructive criticism can be given publicly or privately, depending on the situation and the sensitivity of the topic. You never want to embarrass someone in front of others. If there is even a chance that the criticism may be taken the wrong way, do so in private.

To complete the packaging of the feedback sandwich, use non-verbal communication and techniques of respect. Allow your eyes and body gestures to express your feelings in a positive manner. Pause between your comments of praise and criticism, and control the tone of your voice. Allow the other person the opportunity to respond with his or her feedback. Communication is a two-way street.

When involved in communicating with others, you can decide if you need to use the feedback sandwich process or not, depending on the situation. Most often, it is used in business related communication when issues are being discussed. Listen and study what is being said before responding.

With effective communication skills, you can be assured that what you speak is clearly interpreted. Clear communication and understanding the different parts of effective communication can make daily life go by much easier in many situations. There are three items worth remembering when communicating:

1. Be clear and concise in both written and spoken language. Avoid big words, run-on sentences and unclear phrasing.

2. In certain situations, such as the work environment, keep clear written or audio records of conversations that may need clarification in the future.

3. Keep feedback actionable by giving actionable directions

Make a conscious effort in listening to the way you communicate daily. This may assist you in determining the type of communication hindering words that you may use without realizing it. Even consider asking a close friend or family member for feedback, but remember to be open to the feedback and not take it personally.

Write down the common words that you use that you want to avoid, and think of replacements for it. The replacement words or phrases can be more constructive and positive, rather than authoritative. Once you have established this – practice, practice, practice. You may be well-surprised at the difference this little change can make in your communication with others and how it can improve your life.

Section 3: Time Management Systems

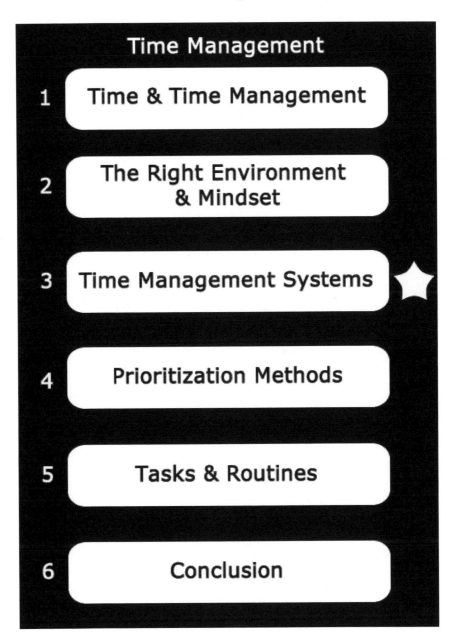

Time Management

1. Time & Time Management
2. The Right Environment & Mindset
3. Time Management Systems
4. Prioritization Methods
5. Tasks & Routines
6. Conclusion

There are many time management systems that automate processes, which eliminate paper work and tedious tasks. In this part of this book we'll discuss 4 well known time management systems.

29. *Getting Things Done (GTD)*

Getting Things Done is a book that was written by David Allen. David Allen is a productivity consultant who helps people learn to organize their lives and manage their time more effectively. His book describes a method he has created that will help anyone become better organized and get more things done in less time. The Getting Things Done method is generally referred to as GTD.

How GTD Works

The GTD method of getting organized, and gaining the ability to effectively manage time operates on a simple premise. The idea behind GTD is that all of us have too much "stuff," as the author calls it, rolling around inside our heads. David Allen defines "stuff" as anything that has no immediate purpose. For instance, a good example of "stuff" is remembering to get an oil change, remembering to pick the kids up from school, and other tasks that we all need to get done each day. According to the author, remembering to do all of these tasks take up too much of our time, and too much of our brainpower.

He says that the way to become more organized is to write things down as soon as the task comes to mind. This means as you think of something that needs done you should write it down on a "to-do" list. You no longer need to spend time remembering to do something because you have written down a reminder. Now you can spend your time thinking about and getting things done. David Allen says that his method makes you look at your life, and your daily, weekly, and monthly tasks on a regular basis. He says this will help you keep on top of all of the things you need to get done, and want to accomplish. The GTD method of becoming organized has pros and cons.

The Benefits of GTD

The first benefit of GTD is that you will have a feeling of relaxed control over your life. By doing regular mind dumps of your "stuff" you will definitely have the feeling that you are taking control of your life, and becoming more efficient and organized.

Next, the GTD method makes you take stock of your life on a frequent basis. If you follow the GTD method you will be required to do a weekly review of the things you have gotten done, and the things you have left to do. You will also need to prioritize your "to-do" list. On top of the weekly reviews you should be adding and removing things from your list on a daily basis, this gives you the ability to do short daily reviews of your life. This can be a useful tool for anyone, and it will make you feel more relaxed because you will see that you are in control of your life and the things you need to get done.

The GTD will give you the freedom of choice. The program gives you the ability to choose what things you do, and when you do them. Those that use the GTD plan like the freedom of choice offered by the program.

Another advantage of using the GTD method of organization is that it will help you to make and keep your commitments. You will also find that you have more time to plan the best way to get things done. You will find that you can now plan in advance, which makes it less stressful when you have a big project coming due in the future. Since you now have the time to pre-plan, you will have confidence knowing you will have time available to complete the big project.

The GTD method will help you create, track, and fulfill your dreams. This is done through the use of what David Allen calls a "someday/maybe" list. This is a list of things you would like to accomplish at some time in the future; you will keep this list along with your to-do list.

Lastly the GTD method will make you more productive, and make it so that you are now doing a better job of managing your time.

Disadvantages of GTD

As with any new program there are disadvantages as well as advantages. Some people say that the GTD method wants you to create too many different habits, making it hard for many people to sustain the program. Those that make this statement do not say this is a shortcoming of the program, but more of a shortcoming in people in general. They say that most people will fall off the GTD wagon before they give the program a chance to make changes in their daily lives.

Some critics of the GTD method claim the method does not give you enough instruction on how to make progress within the program. Some people think David Allen should have given people more guidance on how to get through the lists they have created.

Some people think the big problem with GTD is that some people's list will be too big to handle. Critics say that if someone's list is too big it could cause paralysis, then they will not get anything done. Those that use the program say that your initial lists could be quite large, but if you concentrate on getting things on the list done, before long your lists will shrink to a manageable size.

One of the other things that some people do not like about the GTD system is that if you have one really busy week it can destroy the entire plan. Others have said that the system is too complicated. They blame this shortcoming on the language that is used in the book. Another of the disadvantages of the GTD program is that it is not goal-driven. Critics say that the author starts with a "bottom-up" ideology where you get on top of your daily workload before you give your future goals any thought. Many people think that you should start your list, and start working on the goals in your life, then move on to completing mundane daily tasks.

30. Franklin-Covey

The Franklin Covey Time Management System

What is it?

The Franklin covey time management system is a paper-based planner with daily pages; on one side you have your calendar and your to-do list, and on the other you keep notes. It is regarded as the classic day-at-a-glance planner. This paper-based planner is named after the US president Franklin Benjamin who kept a similar book as described in his autobiography.

The Franklin Planner is made in five sizes that are all ring-bound. The planners differ according to dimensions ranging from micro to monarch which is the largest.

Each section of the Franklin Planner consists of double pages for each day. It also has areas for appointment agendas, prioritized task lists and a dairy page. The Franklin Planner also contains a section for addresses at the rear. It also caters for those who seek to personalize it further by including other inserts such as exercise logs, ledger sheets and other reference materials.

The Franklin Planner seeks to merge appointments and tasks so as to ensure proper and efficient personal information management. The Franklin Covey Time Management System also seeks to cultivate a culture of serious planning at the start of each new day.

How it works:

- Prioritized Daily Task List
  Write all the things you would want to achieve in a particular day in this section. You should then prioritize each listed task according to its importance. There is a column where you classify each task as either A, B, or C.
  A Valuable task that must be completed today.
  B Vital but can be postponed. Should be done today

C Could be done today. You won't lose anything if you postpone.

After assigning the relevant priority, number each task within its category. This will help you know which tasks to handle first.

- Symbol Legend
  The tracking column will help you to identify progress and decide on the relevant action to take. The column can help you identify completed tasks, tasks moved to a future date, tasks assigned to another person, semi-complete tasks and incomplete tasks in your Financial Planner.

- Appointment Schedule
  This section is reserved for recording appointments, dates and meetings.

- Notes Page
  The beauty of this page is that it prevents a scenario of papers lying around that could hamper an individual's schedule and ease of getting things done. This is the place to record miscellaneous details such as meeting notes, journal entries, and phone messages etc. However, remember to number each entry and log it in your Monthly Index. This will make it easier to find when you need it later.

- Monthly Calendar Tabs
  These play a vital role in the retrieval of information. The Monthly Tab helps you to keep a tab on important dates and remember vital information about the date.

- Master Task List
  It is usually on the back of each Monthly Calendar Tab. This is the place to enumerate all the things you would wish to accomplish along the month. Such include renewing memberships and subscriptions. It is important to

refer to this section when creating the daily task list.

- Monthly Index
  In this section, you should summarize all the important
  information collected by date. This will help you when you
  need to retrieve the information at a future date.

- Weekly Compass Card®
  This section essentially helps you to discover the most
  important thing to be done in a particular week. The
  Weekly Compass Card adds meaning to the Franklin Covey
  Time Management System.

Pros

- The Franklin Covey Time Management System uses
  proven principles that will help you attain a balance in your
  life and thus help you to achieve goals and dreams based on
  an established planning process.

- The various exercises incorporated into the Franklin Covey
  Time Management System will enable you to discover the
  kind of person you would like to be, important goals and
  your purpose in life.

- The Franklin Planner will help you to plan for both short-
  term and long-term goals based on the discovered values
  and purpose in life.

- The Franklin Planner helps you to learn to act according to
  priority and urgency of the task. It thus helps you to be
  more productive in your daily routines and assignments. It
  achieves this by allowing you to take the time to
  meticulously plan for daily and weekly plans and schedule
  activities based on priority rather than impulse.

- The Franklin Planner basically helps an individual to focus
  on only the most valued tasks that will help them

accomplish what they want in their life. It thus helps the person using it to be not only productive but also to develop high self-esteem and a sense of fulfillment.

Cons

There has been a decline in the use of the Franklin Planner in modern times. This is mainly due to the fact that the Franklin Planner has in a way failed to fit into the new system of doing work. The part of the Franklin Covey Time Management System that makes it tedious or cumbersome to use is due to the fact that any tasks that are not done one day are carried forward to be done on another time.

This transfer process is what gets to the nerves of most professionals in this day and age. The transfer process gets even more tedious when you have a huge list of things to do on your comparatively less accessible master task list.

People who receive a lot of email messages on a daily basis may also find it difficult and cumbersome to use the Franklin Planner. This is because they will have to transfer a lot of information from their emails into handwritten to-do lists crucial for the traditional Franklin Covey Time Management System.

Therefore the classic Franklin Planner faces stiff competition from time management systems that integrate with email and offer nifty features such as drag and drop.

However, Franklin Covey does sell a software version of its time management system called "PlanPlus for Windows" that seeks to correct some of the cons of the traditional Franklin Planner. The online version of the system is branded as "PlanPlus Online".

Useful Link
http://getorganized.fcorgp.com/guide_to_using_your_planning_sys
tem

31. Anthony Robbins' Rapid Planning Method

Anthony Robbins, one of the world's top self-help experts, has developed a unique plan that people can use for their time management needs. This program is the Anthony Robbins' Rapid Planning Method. It is a plan used to make it easier for anyone to be more productive while getting the best results possible. It could be one of the most valuable programs that anyone might encounter.

What is the Plan?

The plan is used to help make it easier for anyone to get their important tasks in life under control. It is used to allow a person to figure out what can be done in order to feel a sense of achievement while also fulfilling all of the tasks that one has to do.

The plan involves taking a look at purpose as a key part of planning one's actions. This includes working to tap into the purpose and emotional value that comes with it as a means of being more proficient when working. It's done to improve anyone's life and to make the process of living a little easier to work with.

In fact, Robbins feels that the method can be summarized in three parts. These include the plan being results-oriented, purpose-driven and made with taking action in mind over what one can do.

How does it work?

The Rapid Planning Method works with a series of points. First, a person has to think about what that person really wants out of life. This includes something that could be measured. It has to be as exact as possible. This is the first part of setting the method in motion.

The next part is to think about the purpose that comes with the plan. This includes the reasoning for why something needs to be done. It includes thinking about the triggers that might make it a little easier for a person to focus on a particular goal. Part of this involves the use of varying trigger words to make it easier for an action to be utilized the right way.

The next step involves thinking about how to get more actions done. Chunking is a procedure that the Rapid Planning Method uses. It involves figuring out how to put different ideas and concepts into one series of ideas that can be easy for the mind to focus on. Much of this could include thinking about what tasks could be used together to reach some kind of objective. This could work with as many groups as needed but the plan often involves only a few tasks in each individual program.

Another part relates to getting these ideas together into a massive action plan. Everything must be arranged with not only a series of steps but also the purpose that comes with getting these steps taken care of. It all has to be done to make it easier for the participant to go after things and to understand what the plan is really all about.

The process is used to give a person an idea of how to get things done and how to stay motivated when doing so. It has to be done to make it a little easier for anyone to do things the right way no matter what is going on.

What are the Benefits?

The benefits that come with the program are very impressive. First, the program can work well for practically any kind of action. This comes from how the plan caters to those who are able to focus the right way. Focus is needed to make it easier for anyone to be active and more likely to do anything that one puts their mind to.

This is also used to give anyone a sense of purpose. It focuses on why things have to be done and not just how they have to be done. It is a real motivational point that has to work well if something is to be successful.

There is even the benefit of how it can reduce stress. The program is used to organize the things that someone has to do. It makes it a little easier for different actions to be taken care of the right way.

The Rapid Planning Method helps you to see how well tasks can be related to each other. One reason why so many people fail to do what they want to when it comes to handling certain tasks is because they fail to see that some actions can be combined to work in one way. This includes seeing that even the most isolated tasks might have some kind of relationship with other tasks that need to be done at a given time. It's a smart point to find when trying to do things the right way.

What are the Drawbacks?

Anthony Robbins' Rapid Planning Method is useful but it is not without its faults. The program recommends that people who get into it try and work with only a few points at a time. This includes concentrating on only five different points at a time in each objective. This might be used to make it a little easier for actions to work but it also means that it works best for shorter objectives.

The next concern about this is that it often involves working with a set series of parameters at a given time. This includes thinking about what can go on without any real alternatives. It often makes it so new objectives have to be thought of if certain ones don't pan out well.

Where to Go for Details

There are plenty of links that offer information on what Anthony Robbins' Rapid Planning Method is all about. It may help to visit http://www.tonyrobbins.com/products/time-life-management/ first. This is the product section of the official website of Anthony Robbins. It offers additional details on how the system can be used.

This method of productivity may be used to give anyone an opportunity to do the most out of anything. The Rapid Planning Method should be used to give anyone an easier time getting different actions and functions handled as productively as possible, to see how well anything can be done when trying to be more productive and proficient with different activities in life.

32. Pomodoro Technique

The Pomodoro technique is one of the many time management techniques. The technique was developed in the late 1980s by Francesco Cirillo. It makes use of a timer which breaks working time into intervals of 25 minutes each. The intervals are known as Pomodoros, which is an Italian word for 'tomato'. The method has grown in popularity over the years as people get more conscious about time management.

The Pomodoro technique has been applied in pair programming techniques. It is closely related to other time management techniques such as timeboxing. Another closely related technique is the iterative and incremental development technique which is applied in software design. The technique is based on the fact that frequent time breaks improve mental ability.

The implementation of the technique involves 5 basic steps:

- Make a decision about the task to be carried out.

- Set the timer to periods of 25 minutes.

- Perform the task until the timer rings and record with an X.

- Take a brief break of 3-5 minutes.

- After every four Pomodoros, have a longer break of about 15-30 minutes

The Underlying Principles

Planning, visualizing, tracking, recording and processing are all fundamental to the technique. Planning involves the prioritization of the tasks. This is done by recording them in a list of each day's activities. This enables the user to estimate the effort that each task requires. Once each Pomodoro is completed, it is recorded. This adds a positive sense of accomplishment in the mind of the user. It also provides a table of raw data on which the user is motivated to work on and improve.

Generally, one Pomodoro is the equivalent of a time period of 25 minutes. If a task is completed before the time in the Pomodoro it is dedicated to overlearning. The regular breaks that are taken aid assimilation. After each Pomodoro, a short break of 3-5 minutes is taken. After a set of four Pomodoros, a longer break of 15-30 minutes is taken.

One main goal of the technique is to minimize the impact of both external and internal interruptions on flow and focus. A Pomodoro is taken and treated as an indivisible time period. If an interruption occurs during an activity, either the Pomodoro is postponed or the other activity is recorded.

How Can Pomodoro Help You?

The main benefit is that it trains your mind to work in spurts. This increases concentration and results in better work output. Due to its nature and the breaks in between the Pomodoros, it takes much of the pressure off the task. This discourages multitasking which directly enhances the quality of the work output.

If you have a large list of things to do, the technique helps you crank through them faster by making you adhere to your own strict time schedule. As you watch the timer winding down, you are spurred to move on quickly as you can witness the results. As you continue timing your activities, you become more and more accountable for all your tasks. It minimizes the time you would waste through unnecessary procrastination.

The system is very easy to use and the results are manifest from the word go. You can actually note improvements in your work output process within a day. Within 7-20 days, one is able to master the technique fully. The result is a more effective time management program.

The Pros

It makes you a better manager of you own time. Through your subconscious effort to beat deadlines, you become a better time manager. It increases productivity. It improves the quality of work output. It trains your brain to work in spurts making it more effective and efficient in carrying out of tasks. It helps you get motivated and positive about your work

The Cons

Some critics argue that it is sort of ridiculous since one can time himself/herself naturally even without having a timer on the desk. Another criticism is due to the fact that failing to finish a Pomodoro won't allow you to tick it with an X. This may frustrate users especially when interrupted by events that are not their making.

The Pomodoro time management technique is one of a kind. It is effective and efficient. More importantly, it transforms the user to a better time manager and increases both the quality and quantity of the work.

Section 4: Prioritization Methods

Time Management

1. Time & Time Management
2. The Right Environment & Mindset
3. Time Management Systems
4. Prioritization Methods
5. Tasks & Routines
6. Conclusion

Time management strategies are often associated with the recommendation to set personal goals. The literature stresses themes such as: Work in Priority Order - set goals and prioritize.

Goals are recorded and may be broken down into a project, an action plan, or a simple task list. For individual tasks or for goals, an importance rating may be established, deadlines may be set, and priorities assigned. This process results in a plan with a task list or a schedule or calendar of activities.

Following are 4 methods that can help you prioritize your tasks.

33. POSEC Method

For those who are interested in maximizing both their time and effort, they may want to review the POSEC system as a viable method to reach the goals and objectives that they have set for themselves. The POSEC System can be described as a systematic way to manage tasks. It provides each individual with the basic rules and guidelines to place the things they have to accomplish in a more efficient and effective way.

What is the POSEC Time Management System?

The acronym, POSEC stands for Prioritizing, Organizing, Streamlining, Economizing and Contributing. It is known as a time management system that offers a solution to getting better organized by breaking up large projects into smaller personal tasks. Although this type of system is great for many people, it may not be for everyone to use, meaning each individual should review the system closely to see if they could apply it to the projects that they have to accomplish.

One of the best features included in POSEC is placing things that must be accomplished first in the order of their importance, which is part of Maslow's Needs Hierarchy principles. Functions that make up the POSEC system of time management are listed below:

- Prioritize.
  Based on an individual's personal goals and objectives (business and personal) all of the daily tasks involved should be defined and then prioritized by their order of importance. This is also the step that involves allocating a specific time frame for each individual task.

- Organize.
  After the tasks have been prioritized in order of importance, another function involves getting organized. For example, the person must have structure in this process. Working on a desk or in any environment that is not organized can

impede progress keeping it from being efficient. Also, when meeting others to accomplish these goals, arriving on time is essential. Hence, a calendar to schedule appointments will be needed to keep every element of the project working together.

- Streamline Tasks.
  Sometimes people may use a long method to complete a task instead of saving time. When an individual is adhering to the principles contained in POSEC, they will have to streamline the tasks involved by finding the best ways to save both time and effort.

- Economize.
  Economizing is also essential to following the principles of POSEC. Identifying and performing only the essential steps in the task is one of the best ways to economize. This may involve learning new skills to accomplish certain tasks. For example, if an individual is using old manual bookkeeping methods to calculate their budget, they should learn how to use some of the most recent bookkeeping software instead.

- Contribute.
  While some people tend to do things that increase their personal satisfaction only, others add tasks on the list that will allow them to contribute what they have learned or earned to their communities. However, to adhere to POSEC guidelines, contribution to others must always be included in the goals and objectives that people set.

POSEC is known as a popular method of time management. For many people, it is a proven and effective time management system. One of its main focuses is on putting first things first. By placing things that people want to achieve in a hierarchy order, they can start achieving their major goals and objectives by breaking them up into one task at a time.

This management time system allows the individual to accomplish these tasks on a daily basis, since it keeps them focused on completing each task by a certain time. Once the first task is complete, the person can move on to the next task, while also working within a set time frame. This system gives the individual a systematic way of achieving the goals and objectives by a certain time frame. By breaking large projects down into small tasks, they are easier to achieve.

Efficiency is also embedded into the process because it allows the individual to focus on eliminating steps in the tasks that are not necessary. When eliminating unnecessary steps, this system helps to save both time and extra effort. This management system provides an individual with a way to accomplish all of their goals and objectives in a minimal amount of time.

34. The Urgent/Important Matrix

More and more people started to realize the benefits of the Eisenhower model time management matrix. The history tells us that the distinction between important and urgent was first drawn by US President Dwight D Eisenhower. He managed to have one of the most simple and yet most powerful approaches to personal time management. Also called the Urgent/Important matrix, this tool can help you manage your time in a much better way.

What is it and How Does it Work?

Eisenhower was a very busy man, so in order to better planify his time, he started to study which tasks are important and which ones are urgent. Importance and urgency are usually two different aspects of a task, and we need to make a difference between them in order to save time when planning.

The Eisenhower matrix is a powerful tool when it comes to thinking about prioritizing tasks. The truth is that we all have to deal with many problems and tasks each day, and they consume a lot of our important time. Therefore, we need a tool to help us manage our time more effectively. If you use a to-do list or a day-planner, you probably know how helpful it is to make use of a time management tool. However, none of them even comes close to the Eisenhower model time management.

A good time management means being efficient and effective in the same time. If you want to manage your time more effectively and to achieve all those necessary things, you need to spend your time on important things rather than urgent. In order to minimize the stress of those tight deadlines, you have to understand the difference between urgent and important tasks. While urgent activities demand more attention in the near future and are usually associated with the achievement of somebody else's goals, important activities will always have an outcome that will lead to the achievement of your own goals and plans. Unfortunately, we usually focus on urgent activities rather than important ones, without realizing the opportunities we lose.

The matrix is composed of four categories, each of one representing one quadrant.

1. Urgent and important tasks: these are usually those things we turn our attention to in the first place, ignoring all others. Some examples include: an important call from a potential customer, your kitchen catching fire, a baby crying, a deadline to submit your tax reports or a printer breakdown when an important report is due.

2. Urgent, but not important: these are usually distractions or interruptions that are extremely important to someone else. For example, Facebook updates, washing the dishes or a call from your friend who asks you to go shopping for him are urgent, but not important. If they will take too much of your time, you might end up feeling miserable and stressed.

3. Important, but not urgent: these are those tasks that are the most beneficial to you. The more important, but not urgent tasks we can accomplish, the better we will feel about ourselves. Tasks like working on a project, going to the gym or learning for an exam are just some of the hundreds of activities we can practice to improve the way we think, look and act.

4. Not urgent and not important: these tasks are usually a waste of time, since they will rob us of productive time. Try to avoid spending too much time online, browsing the web or checking your Facebook timeline.

Since you have only a limited amount of time each day, you need to prioritize your tasks. It is obvious that the first priority goes to important and urgent tasks. The second one should always be important, not urgent tasks, rather than not important and urgent ones. The truth is that we seldom forget about time management, and we end up watching a movie or chatting on Skype rather than working on a project or cooking.

If you want to gain peace of mind, you spend your time according to your priorities and don't waste a second. It is important to try to apply Eisenhower's Matrix in your everyday life. Think of it as a professional time management tool that will help you become the person you've always wanted to be. By the way, president Eisenhower successfully managed his daily activities, which weren't few, and because of that, he became one of the most famous people in history.

35. 80/20 Rule / ABC Analysis

Good time management requires the understanding of the 80/20 rule. Often referred to as the Pareto Principle, the 80/20 rule says there is rarely a balance between input and output. In relation to work force, this rule means that approximately 20 percent of one's efforts results in 80 percent of production. Leaning to first notice, then focus on that 20 percent is the main factor in making the most effective use of one's time.

Time management is important to any career you hold, in using your talent to its fullest potential. It is the main factor in taking your effort and matching it to your given skills. The majority of successful people world-wide attribute the 80/20 rule to their accomplishments.

In 1906, Vilfredo Pareto, an intelligent and highly-regarded economist in Italy, created a mathematical formula to demonstrate the difference in the allocation of wealth in his country. In his studies, he observed the 20 percent of the Italian population owned 80 percent of the country's wealth.

This principle has become a valuable tool to assist in the effective management of one's life. Whether it was used to manage a career or other items in your life, this principle was designed to effectively gain success in all areas of life. There is no limit to the possibilities in using this principle.

Definition of the 80/20 Rule

The simple definition of this rule is that it clarifies that the 80 percent of what you produce (your outcome) directly comes from 20 percent of your actions (your input). In the use of Pareto's formula, this rule has been proven factual in every aspect of life.

In the management of your life, sometimes it doesn't matter what exact figures you use to measure your input and outcome. The most essential thing to remember is that your life journey consists of many actions included in the defined 20 percent. This gives credit to the 80 percent majority of your happiness, success, and outcome.

This means that 20 percent of what you do, or what you produce, generates 80 percent of your total income. This means that for you to continuously produce income (80 percent), you need to ensure that appropriate attention is given towards the 20 percent that you do have.

The Keys to Importance of the 20 Percent

- Focus – This is needed in order for you to produce quality with your actions and in the generation of income. Once you give your focus to the task at hand, you will produce great results in terms of income and productivity.

- Organization – Organize your work space, such as your desk, and your time. Do not complete any task without developing a plan, as this is where wasting time and effort manifests.

- Productivity – The first step in productivity is knowing your goal – knowing what needs to be achieved. Keep your goals in mind and the steps you need to take to get there. Allow your goals to be your motivation. This simple process will turn you into an exceptionally productive person.

- Being Wise – Choose to work wisely and appropriately. Do not just work and work for nothing. Work on the tasks that are profitable. Prioritize tasks and make wise decisions about the use of your time and energy. Do the things that need to be done first according to deadlines or needs.

- Giving your Best – Simply give your best in all things you do. This is the best approach to all of life's options and situations. By doing your best, everything will flow in the correct pattern. When working on a task, pretend that it's your last chance to prove yourself – to accomplish something. Make the end result the best that you have through completeness, preciseness, and directness. Make doing your best a habit.

Understanding and practicing the 80/20 Rule is the key to you experiencing success in every area of your life. Use these skills and success is yours for the taking.

The alternative term often used in conjunction with Pareto Principle is ABC analysis which stems from the fact that the first 20% of important items are known as Category A items; the next, typically 40%, are Category B items and the relatively unimportant, though larger in number, 40% are Category C items.

It is a form of Pareto analysis in which the items such as: activities, customers, documents, inventory items and sales territories are grouped into three categories (A, B, and C) in order of their estimated importance. 'A' items are very important, 'B' items are important, 'C' items are marginally important.

For example, the best customers who yield highest revenue are given the 'A' rating, are usually serviced by the sales manager, and receive most attention. 'B' and 'C' customers warrant progressively less attention and are serviced accordingly.

36. IPA's versus NIPA's

One of the greatest benefits of living in an open, democratic environment is that you have, within reason, total control of virtually infinite choices over the conduct and quality of your own life. You have probably heard the cliché, "you can be anything you want to be," dispensed to you as well-meaning advice by your peers and elders. Paradoxically, the source of an individual's greatest strengths -- free will and a level playing field -- may turn out to be the very same source of a glaring weakness: the ease entertaining a variety of ideas and actions, and losing focus of the important things that lead to success, achievement, fulfillment and happiness.

You can simplify life as a string of decisions that result in actions you take that lead to certain consequences. Each action you decide to take is like a little prod that steers you along a different direction as you hurtle along through life. It follows that you can control the direction of your life by deciding on which outcomes you would like to realize for yourself; these are your goals.

Consequently, to realize them you need to consciously steer yourself toward the general direction of your goals. The actions that keep you in sight of your objectives are called Income Producing Activities or IPAs. In this context, though, 'income' refers to more than simply money earning; it also encompasses anything that may be of value to you. In essence, 'income' can be equated to your dreams and goals. An IPA is any action you take or activity you engage in that brings you closer to your goals. Any other action that steers you away from the prize is a Non-Income Producing Activity, or NIPA.

Using this metaphor in real life, consider how you spend your day. What activities fill your day and demand your time, talent and energy? Does each activity steer you toward the goals you have set for yourself? With each little accomplishment you chalk up, do you find yourself a little bit closer to your objectives? If your answer is yes, then congratulations! It may take you some time, or it may take you no time at all, but in the end, these IPAs will help you realize your goals, dreams and objectives. The secret to fulfilling your dreams is to focus on IPAs.

Of course this is easier said than done. In real life, although you may have set clear goals for yourself, and even if you intend to stay steadfast and focused on your prize it is not easy to keep on course all the time. Distractions abound, and these can easily entice you to veer away from your IPAs. And it is not as if you can easily brush distractions aside and continue on toward your goals without missing a beat. The reason many distractions succeed in distracting is precisely because they are often enticing and seductive. The human mind is wired to search for what is pleasurable, so you easily succumb to the wiles of the fun and the easy.

Another reason IPAs may fail is because of obstacles and challenges. The easy part about goals is defining them. The tough part is when you actually reach for your goals and discover that someone else has his sights on the same prize. Or when you discover that the prize is in a three-foot concrete vault at the bottom of the ocean guarded by a school of sharks. These obstacles may be no more than minor irritations that put you in a foul mood as you perform your IPAs, but some of them will prove to be seemingly immovable barriers that will use up your energy and resources and put in question your commitment and character. These are the obstacles that have the power to stop you dead in your tracks and set you off in another direction in pursuit of some other dream.

What can you do to keep your goals in focus, succeed at executing your IPAs (while minimizing the distraction of NIPAs) and keep yourself moving toward your objectives?

Here are a few handy tips:

- Keep your goals in focus. You need to start with clear and unambiguous objectives. It helps to write your goals down and to visualize them with your very own vision board. Review your goals every chance you get, and quickly

130

assess how much further you need to go to achieve it. Constantly remind yourself of your prize.

- Make a plan. If you have a plan that incorporates your IPAs, it makes it much easier to attain your goals. Create milestones that act like steps up a ladder toward your prize.

- Marry your priorities. They are your primary focus.

- Work your plan. As the popular sneaker ad says, "Just do it!" Go and execute your IPAs.

- Recognize distractions and obstacles. Always ask if something you are thinking of doing will contribute toward your goal. If it will, it is an IPA worth doing.

- Know your 'Avoid at all Cost List' and stick to it. Not doing so is the type of behavior that creates some of the most detrimental distractions in making big things happen.

- Motivate yourself to move forward, especially when confronted by distractions and obstacles. Get help when you need it, and keep a tight schedule to keep you on track. When you find your energy dipping, engage in an activity that will re-energize you. Approach seemingly tough problems from a different angle or perspective.

Section 5: Tasks & Routines

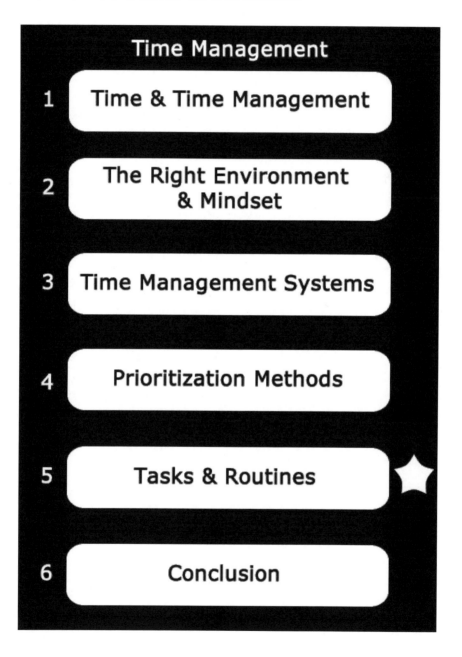

37. Checklists

While goal and task lists can help you remember everything that you have to do, using checklists for repetitive tasks can make you be more productive as well. The more complex the task is ahead of you, the more useful a checklist becomes.

You may think it's odd to spend your valuable time making a checklist how to finish a job you've completed many times before. Such a list however can become a useful blueprint that will eventually save you time and ensure a constant quality of your output.

So you'll have more time to work through the things that you don't have to do frequently.

There's a reason why airline pilots use checklists to help them through complex processes like landing and takeoffs. Otherwise, they would have to rely on their memory to determine if they've taken all the necessary steps and human error, fatigue, and distraction could become serious problems.

In the case of tasks that you perform often but not every day, a checklist can serve as basic instructions. For example if you build Wordpress websites with numerous details you have to think about with each build it'll come in very handy if you can use a checklist detailing all the necessary steps as your guide. Just mark off all the finished items till you have them all. That way you wouldn't waste precious time trying to figure it out each time you have to do it.

In addition to helping you remember things that could cause problems if forgotten, a checklist can help you move forward to your chosen goals, by making sure you take action consistently. The way to reach a goal is by working at it every single day, even for a small amount of time.

By sticking to a daily habit using checklists, you'll gain the experience to become an expert in no time at all. You can use them for exercise, writing, learning something new, like programming or a foreign language, to get better at your job, build a business, etc.

38. Task Lists (To-Do's)

Time management tasks in relation to implementation of goals frequently centers on the management of task lists. A task list (also to-do list or things-to-do) is a list of tasks to be completed, such as chores or steps toward completing a goal. It is an inventory tool which serves as an alternative or supplement to memory.

Task lists are used in self-management, grocery lists, business management, project management, and software development. It may involve more than one list. When one of the items on a task list is accomplished, the task is checked or crossed off. The traditional method is to write these on a piece of paper with a pen or pencil, usually on a note pad or clip-board.

Numerous digital equivalents are now available, including PIM (Personal information management) applications and most smartphones. There are also several web-based task list applications, many of which are free.

A to-do list is a fundamental tool for getting things done: it helps you plan your day, see what you've accomplished, and what you should work on next. But a badly-written to-do list can actually sabotage your productivity instead of boost it.

The best part of using a to-do list is crossing items off of it as done, finished, complete. Some tasks are easier to tick off as done than others, so you want to make your to-do list as doable as possible. A common mistake is assigning ourselves impossible tasks that never get done because we didn't think them through. If you put in some thought up front, you can pare down your to-do list to the tasks you're most likely to check off the list.

First, know the difference between a project, goal, and a task. A project is a big undertaking that involves several tasks.

Main Reasons to use a To Do list:

- To better manage your time

- To ensure that you won't forget anything

- To "zoom out" to see the big picture

- To "zoom in" to focus on a specific part of your work

Making a to-do list is really simple. Just write down everything that you need to do. Consider everything, no matter how small the task is.

List all projects and tasks and sub divide them into categories such as important/unimportant or urgent/non- urgent. Must this project or task be completed? Is it vital to the running of your household? Would the world end if it wasn't done?

If you are finished jotting down all of the tasks that you need to work on during the entire day, the next thing you're going to do is allocate the time to do it all. Assign a time to do the task on the day. It should not always be the exact time. An estimated time on how much is going to probably take is enough already. And also, when assigning the time, make sure it is sensible.

————Sidebar —

If you are faced with a vaguely-defined, open-ended list of tasks, you can feel a sense of hopelessness and your energy drops. You can even find yourself paralyzed by inaction when faced with 3 or 4 really exciting pieces of work if you don't think there's time to do them all.

You need to give yourself room to breathe!

Faced with the twin problems of unpredictable interruptions and the Sisyphus effect of never-ending tasks, you need to give yourself room to breathe, keep a clear head and stay focused on what you want to achieve. In short, you need to install a buffer between others' demands and your response. Otherwise you'll end up in permanently anxious and unproductive 'reaction mode'.

On the other hand, you need to find a way of fulfilling your commitments and giving others what they need from you within a reasonable timescale. Otherwise you'll quickly gain a reputation for unreliability and pay the penalty.

Give yourself rewards for all your hard work. Designate rewards such as a long, hot bath, a power nap or viewing an hour's worth of your favorite television program, as a reward for cleaning out your closet, organizing a junk drawer or weeding out your filing cabinet. Play music while you're working, for fun and energy.

Now, to make it more fun and to be effective, introduce yourself to the beauty of crossing things out. Always cross out the tasks that you complete. Crossing out finished tasks will boost your morale.

Then establish priorities. Identify the tasks that need to be done today, tomorrow, next week, etc. Identify also which of the tasks that are mandatory appointments and arrange the tasks according to urgency. Write down first the tasks that have high urgency and then write the least urgent tasks.

39. *Prioritize*

Obviously before prioritizing you have to already know what is important in your life and where you want to devote attention and focus. Applying sole attention to what outside entities have agreed on as a priority (this can be work, family, or even friends), and not to what you feel is more important, is a surefire way to not pay attention to your calling. In fact, this difference between what is important to you and what is important to other entities is grounds to grow some awesome resentment, produce little, and procrastinate.

Prioritizing is about making choices. Here are ideas to help you prioritize.

- To prioritize effectively, you need to be able to recognize what is important. So you have to know what you want. The important (high priority) tasks are based on what you value and those that help you achieve your goals and provide meaningful and rewarding long-term results. Consciously choosing the right things to do based on the results that you want to achieve. As you perform different tasks, think about where they fit on your priority list.

- Making a list of all the tasks that need to be done is a good way to begin prioritizing. Prioritize the items on the list by using the ABC method to rank your priorities. For example, Priority A: Must Do (crucial tasks and commitments to do today), Priority B: Should Do (important things that do not need to be done today), and Priority C: Nice to Do (least urgent tasks).

- Do not think of your priorities as just jobs that need to be done. Instead of just doing whatever pops up, you consciously choose what you are going to do and what you are not going to do. As you remind yourself to direct yourself to the most important tasks first, you will find yourself letting go of tasks that really didn't need to be done at that time.

- Also take note of the difference between tasks that you need to do and those that you want to do. Deciding the order in which you prioritize tasks means you start with the needs first and move to the wants afterwards.

- When you prioritize unplanned activities, keep your goals in mind and rely on your instincts. Your effectiveness in prioritizing in these situations depends on the clarity of your goals.

- When prioritizing, you need to be able to separate the tasks that need doing from the busy work that tends to eat away at your time. Many tasks that fill up your day may not need doing at all or could be done less frequently. Determine what that busy work is in your career and your life.

- Keep in mind that everything in your life cannot be a priority. There are many important things that will compete for attention over your lifetime and there are not enough hours in that lifetime to give attention to everything good and worthwhile. You have to be selective. Prioritize and consciously choose what to do (and what not to do) so you don't get overwhelmed trying to get everything done.

- Develop systems to help keep things running smoothly. Many times that can be accomplished by using a personal calendar. In family settings, a master calendar is helpful.

- Rank and label items according to priority. Make a to-do list for the day. Include some high, medium, and low priority items daily to help ensure many important projects are getting completed.

- Also, try to figure out what time of the day you are most productive and alert. If you are able to figure this one out, write in this time the tasks that are a bit demanding and a bit difficult too. It is during this time of day that you will be most productive. Furthermore, after finishing a difficult task, always pair it with the easy ones. Or after doing a very long task, pair it with short ones. By doing this, it can help you accomplish a lot of tasks during the day.

- In addition to this, allow yourself some time to unwind or take a break.

- Use technology to help you prioritize tasks. Sometimes an important task can be done more quickly with the use of technology. Instead of conducting an appointment in person, can you do it through a conference call or by e-mail?

- When prioritizing, make sure to include deadlines for each task. It will make tasks easier to prioritize and give you more focus.

Prioritize 'important but not urgent' work.

In his book The Seven Habits of Highly Effective People, Stephen Covey classifies work tasks according to whether they are important or urgent.

	URGENT	Not urgent
IMPORTANT	Urgent and important	Important but not urgent
Not important	Urgent but not important	Not urgent and not important

Covey points out that many of us spend too much time on tasks that are urgent and important – in other words, staving off emergencies by rushing around to solve problems or responding to others' demands at short notice.

Covey's solution is to prioritize work that is important but not urgent (the upper right square in the diagram). Though this is hard to do on any given day, it is the only way to ensure you are making progress towards your own goals and dreams, instead of merely reacting to what other people throw at you. And over time, the more you deal with important things before they become urgent, the fewer 'urgent and important' tasks you will have to deal with.

The most obvious way to do this is to work on your own projects/goals first every day, even if it's only for half an hour. Whatever interruptions come along later, you will at least have the satisfaction of having made some progress towards your own goals. Start by working on the goal you want more than anything – the one that has the absolute highest priority to you.

40. Streamline Your Tasks

Always look for ways to streamline your tasks, both on the job and at home. You will accomplish more in less time, so you will reach your goals faster and have more and better quality time for family, recreation and leisure.

Following are a few suggestions to get you started:

Streamline tasks on the job.

Here's how to deal with the ongoing paper mountain on your desk.

- Throw it away. You should throw a paper away as soon as you pick it up and notice you can do without it.

- Could you delegate it to someone? Give it away.

- Next, make three piles of papers.
  1. In the closest pile are items that should be acted upon.
  2. In the next pile are items to be filed. Save them till the end of the day instead of filing them one at a time. It's a great time saver. (Save even more time—delegate the filing once a day.)
  3. In the last pile are papers to be read. If you don't want to read a whole magazine, just copy or tear out the relevant pages. Recycle the rest of it.

If most of your tasks are handled on a computer, then take a few minutes to back-up your data regularly and store it in a safe place. It can take days to recover what you have not backed up.
If you have a work mailbox or e-mail, do not give your addresses to anyone who isn't immediate family or associated with your business. This will save you time, and keep you organized.

Streamline tasks at home.

The more you streamline necessary tasks at home, the more time you will have for family activities. The following suggestions are easy to do and effective.

As at work, we also have paper piles at home. When you receive bills or other important papers in the mailbox, be sure to deal with them swiftly. If you receive junk mail, toss it. Junk mail has nothing to offer us. Do the same with e-mails.

Never put garbage anywhere. More so, don't let these unnecessary objects hide inside your car, cabinets, closets, or under your bed until they become little monsters of their own.

Clean as you go. Always follow the "on the fly" philosophy: close an open drawer when you pass by it, empty a full wastebasket, pick up a clothing item lying on the floor and hang it up. This is a simple way to streamline your tasks as well as maintain a habit of cleanliness. You may involve other people in this habit too.

41. Lists

Many people use daily to-do lists already. The fact is that they can really improve productivity and make it easier to reach our daily goals. On the other hand, the list may also prevent us from keeping an eye on our long-term goals and projects.

It is always good to consider that this list is not just a stand-alone daily schedule, but serves as a part of a bigger arrangement. This bigger arrangement involves using a "Master Goal List" and "Weekly Project List" along with your daily to do list.

1. Master Goal List: it is the most important part of the structure that contains the goals that you want to accomplish within 3 to 6 months. Basically, it should consist of all major improvements that you need to make within the given time frame. Therefore, it will be about the actual purpose of everything that you are planning. Your entire daily activities should mainly revolve around the ideas written on it. In other words, Master Goal list is basically a well-organized list that contains the goals to accomplish and when to accomplish them.

2. Weekly Project List: it is the second part of the structure that should be a guide for you to take important steps to arrive to the real success. Any major accomplishment planned on Master Goal list should be divided into smaller parts. Weekly Project list will make it easier for you to notice the changes or small improvements before the actual purpose is achieved. You can also use this as the reference for the daily to-do lists.

3. Daily To-Do List: the last part of the structure is daily-to-do list. All ideas written on the previously mentioned lists must be turned into many practical matters. Daily to-do list must contain the smallest steps that will eventually lead to the major goals. It basically tells you how to accomplish the real success little by little.

Daily To-Do List will lead you to achieve the goals written on the Weekly Project (the 2nd list of the structure); the small improvements, which are noticeable from the Weekly Project, will notify that in fact you are getting closer to the big accomplishment planned on Master Goal list.

Final Result

Such method is rather unconventional, but when the rules are strictly followed, the result can be impressively surprising. It will basically turn your daily to-do list into the smallest part of the big picture. Accordingly, the list will contain only easy tasks to complete on a daily basis. The long-term purposes written on the Master Goal list are the actual goals and you must focus mainly on them. Overall, thanks to such structure, the daily to-do list will not only consist of some ordinary activities to complete, but it has many important steps to take to improve your life.

42. Scheduling Your Time

With proper scheduling, you can feel less stress and more in control of your life. Here are some tips to refine your scheduling skills:

- Realize that there are boundaries with a schedule. For example, try thinking of your daily schedule as a container that can only be filled with a limited amount of tasks. It is easy to realize that you need to be very selective about deciding which tasks will be placed in the container.

- Do not overschedule yourself and do not schedule items up to the minute, as you want to always leave room for events, meetings, or tasks running over the scheduled time. Build cushions of time in-between your schedule to allow for unexpected events. For example, it is often recommended that financial planners not schedule more than two or three hours of work within an eight-hour period. This is because a financial planner needs to be able to respond immediately to clients when needed.

- Schedule personal time every day for you. The only way to ensure that you have time for you is to schedule it daily.

- Schedule breaks during the day to prevent you from becoming overwhelmed. You will not receive effective time management solutions if you can't function at your full potential. Even taking a power nap of 20 minutes during the day can give you that extra energy to complete your scheduled tasks. Taking time out during the day to clear your mind and relax is a great way to stay focused on the goals identified in your schedule. You may be surprised by new and creative ideas that come to you during these break sessions.

- Crossing off completed tasks. After each scheduled task is completed, cross it off from your list. This is a great way to provide you with a feeling of accomplishment and satisfaction.

- Plan for tomorrow, today. Take time at the end of each day to list and schedule tasks that weren't completed and need to be done the next day. This includes other items that came up during the day that need to be completed or scheduled. This planning allows you to have a smooth transition in the morning when you start your day. You won't have to decide what has to be done first, as everything will already be listed.

Planning your day in advance is not only a skill of being organized, but will increase your ability to complete your tasks on time. When planning your day ahead of time, you know what to expect and what is of importance. This allows you to keep your focus on the tasks that need to be accomplished, and know what can wait until the following day. You will remain on task and reach your goals with great ease.

Acknowledging what needs to be done the next day, can also help you identify any problems that may come your way and possible alternatives or solutions. Unnecessary tasks will also have no room on your schedule; therefore, not affecting your time management. For example, in your personal life you may have the following business day scheduled to pay bills, and then a good friend invites you to coffee. You could easily readjust your schedule and have coffee, or reschedule the coffee invitation. Planning ahead allows you this freedom.

Friday Afternoon Scheduling Tip

Every Friday afternoon of a five day work week, take time to plan your schedule for the following week. By reviewing your schedule on Friday afternoon, you will have a clear idea of what you have completed and what still needs to be completed in the following week.

This process allows you to mentally review your schedule through the weekend so you will be well-prepared on Monday when you start your new work week. Starting your week will be much easier with a distinctive plan of what is to be expected. Here are the specific steps in completing your Friday afternoon scheduling:

- Step One: Complete the list of all the upcoming tasks for the next week, updating your master goal list, weekly project list and to do list. Review your calendar often to review the past week and upcoming week to ensure that all-important tasks are accounted for.

- Step Two: Transformation of your tasks into action pieces. Any tasks not identified as action pieces need to be transformed into action pieces.

- Step Three: Commitments should be pre-scheduled. Pre-schedule and block time on your calendar for set commitments, such as meetings.

- Step Four: Take tasks from step two and place on calendar. Take all your tasks and block time on your calendar for its completion, even if it's just an estimated time. Tasks need to be placed into specific time frames on a calendar to ensure it is not forgotten or put off endlessly.

- Step Five: Remove tasks that will not fit into your calendar. This can be a difficult step, but by making this decision in advance of a new week, you can ensure that the most important tasks are completed in a timely manner. These minor tasks can be divided into three areas – defer, delegate, and delete. Tasks that do not fit in your calendar must be addressed in one of these three areas.

- Step Six: Implementation. When you begin your work week, you can rest assured that you will be focused and on task. You will not have to guess what needs to be done, as it will already be planned out for you on your calendar.

In planning your week in advance, you can be sure that the most important tasks will be completed in a timely manner, while still having room for your personal time. It allows you to prioritize and make necessary decisions at the beginning of the week. Since the important tasks will already be scheduled, you will be more relaxed and focused during the week.

At times, it is necessary to accept the limitations that are placed on us by time. During particular moments in our lives, we may feel that there is not enough time in a day to complete everything that we need to complete. For example, if you have young children, managing your time at home and time at work can be very challenging. This is where we need to acknowledge that we have limited time so tasks or activities that are less important may need to be omitted to make room for the essential items.

Maybe in some circumstances, you may need to minimize your total working hours. This may mean you need to simplify your schedule to limit your tasks and activities. For example, in your personal family life, you may be able to plan meals that are simpler to prepare and adjust the amount of activities that you commit to.

To schedule and manage your time effectively, your time must be balanced. Prioritization of your goals is important, but your time must be equally divided for work, family, friends, rest, and relaxation. This gives you a complete life with less chance of a burn out.

It is okay to schedule activities that you enjoy and that bring you relaxation. These are the things that will make you more productive at work and more fulfilled in your life.

43. Routines

An integral part of making your goal setting and time management a success is to implement some routines. There's no point capturing all those to-do items unless you're going to do something with them – which means regularly reviewing your commitments and deciding what to do.

- It's important to set aside time to think about how you're going to approach your work. It's tempting to 'get going' first thing in the morning, so you feel like you're getting things done – but whenever I do this, my day is always less productive and more stressful than on days where I take 10 minutes to review my commitments and decide how I'm going to tackle them.

- It helps when you step back and see the 'bigger picture' of your work, weigh up priorities and make decisions about the next steps.

- Whenever you review your upcoming work and are confident you can get it all done, it will be a weight off your mind and your energy level will rise. If you review and find that you are not confident of getting it all done, then the review will be even more valuable – better to find out now than later on!

Daily Routine

First, check what tasks need to be done that day, and organize enough time for doing them. See if you have appointments or meetings scheduled that will require your time.

Next, check what tasks are required for the next few days in case you'll have to do some planning for them today. You should then consider what other tasks or major goals you might need to write, to keep propelling you toward your objectives.

Remember, you should always have enough tasks on your plate to keep you going forward, without wearing yourself out. If you don't, it will either mean you are not achieving your major goals, or perhaps that you've sold yourself short by setting objectives that are not dynamic enough for you.

Review your goals. These will keep your mind on what it is you are after and why. It is also a good idea to have a look back, from time to time, at the tasks you've recently completed. There is nothing more inspiring, or rewarding, than to be reminded of the progress you've already made.

When you've done your review, funnel the tasks down to size, and then complete all the tasks you are supposed to. Check them off when finished, and write down any new ones you've come up with.

Although it might seem surprising now, you'll relish setting more major goals and tasks. That's because success is pleasantly addicting. Once you've had a little taste of it, you'll want more because you enjoy the thrill of success.

——————Sidebar——————
Start Your Week on Sunday

You could go into Monday with less of a sense of burden and in a more relaxed and open state of mind. What if you could have already accomplished some of the things that were really important to you by the time Monday arrived?

Your flow won't get interrupted – and that's going to boost your productivity significantly just on its own.

Weekly Routine

While you can't prevent the unexpected, you can lower the chances of it affecting you and your goal-setting routine. You do this through a weekly review that is one part planning and one part troubleshooting.

This weekly review should be done before you start your work week, and include input from your family. You should begin the weekly review by going through your goals—short-term and long-term—giving particular attention to the tasks you need to accomplish that week. While a daily review reminds you of the tasks need doing, if you've not planned ahead for them on a weekly basis they might surprise you, and that can be stressful – particularly if you haven't set time aside for them.

By reviewing at the start of the week, you'll be better able to schedule and plan your tasks, which lessens your stress, ensures successful task completion, and even reduces the amount of time you'll be spending on each task.

The family is the source of most people's enjoyment, but they can also be the source of most unexpected demands on your time. The time demands are particularly stressful when you've got a lot planned. Although it won't entirely eliminate the unexpected, planning your week in advance with your family's input will lower the chances of something unexpected coming up, and lessen its effect on you.

As you schedule your tasks in advance, ask your family what demands they'll have on your time for the upcoming week, and then plan your tasks around your family responsibilities, instead of organizing your tasks first and being surprised, and unprepared, when something else comes up.

Remember, though, always ask your family as positively as possible. You don't want them ever feeling concerned about making demands on your time. And it won't be a concern to you. With proper planning you'll have more than enough time for your job, your family, and for completing all your tasks.

If you haven't yet, mark off the goals you have achieved during the week and add any new goals for the coming week. Measure the progress of each goal so that you are clear about how far you have come and how far there is left to go.

- Organize your work space.

- Gather and process all your 'stuff'

- Review your system

- Update your lists

- Get clean, clear, current and complete

Monthly Routines

Review the progress toward all of your goals as they relate to your mission and vision statements. Make sure you examine goals in all areas of your life. It is important to maintain a healthy balance between your business and personal goals. Review your successes. Take account of your current state of affairs.

Quarterly or Half-Yearly

Review your mission and vision statements in relationship to your roles, values and goals, and adjust where necessary. Don't be reluctant to go back to an earlier step and change a long-term goal or reevaluate your mission – by doing so you will be continually fine-tuning your direction.

Below is a routine overview form you may find helpful. Feel free to copy it or make a similar one yourself for easy reference.

Daily

Check what tasks need to be done today
Check what appointments you have today
Keep an eye on your goals

Work!

Weekly

Review last week's progress
Discuss with family or friends
Review your goals
Adjust if necessary

Monthly

Review your progress toward all of your goals
Review your mission statement
Look at your current state of affairs
Adjust if necessary

Quarterly or Half-Yearly

Review your mission and vision in relationship to your roles,
values and goals

Evaluation

You should evaluate your efforts regularly to be sure you are on
the right track. When you evaluate, remember you are not judging
the person (yourself) but merely checking if you are doing the right
thing and if you are thinking the right thoughts.

You should never be afraid to change routines, goals, missions,
visions or thoughts if new ones work better for you. Perhaps you
meet an unexpected obstacle on your way to meeting your long-
term goal. Reassess and decide if you can adapt your action plan. If
you cannot adapt your plan you will need to consider why the plan
went off course—did you have less power to control the situation
than you initially thought? Were you unaware of some of the
resources you needed and their cost or time obligations?

Use this new information to reconsider your goal. Is it still attainable or do you need to adjust it—either by lengthening the time or changing the outcome—and devise a new action plan?

44. How to Make Sure You Follow Through

Ideas are truly powerful. They can be the building blocks of an empire or they can just be distractions keeping an entrepreneur from accomplishing his real goals. Ideas are much like plants. If you do not nurture them they may simply wither away and die, never seeing the light of day. So how can you avoid this? You can avoid this by knowing what destroys good ideas. Usually, it is not just one cause alone, but a combination of causes. It begins with the best intentions but with no clear plan to follow up, the ideas may come very close to completion but then remain in a state of "almost finished but not completely." Here is how to make sure that you follow through and see your endeavors through to the end:

1: Finish What You Start

Do not simply start a project, start it knowing you intend to complete it. This may sound easy, but in today's world there are a plethora of distractions just waiting to steal your valuable attention. Begin your projects with a true intention of completing them. Know what it takes to finish the job. Just by shifting your perspective this way you will be much more likely to create an action plan and follow through with it.

2: Be Sure To Allocate Time

Many a task list is created without any thought being given to how long it will take to complete each item. Be sure to allocate time to ensure that you do actually follow through. Get into a habit of setting a time to complete each task and you will automatically move projects to the back burner if you do not have the time to complete them right now.

3: Create A System For Managing Ideas

You may have tons of great ideas, but it can be overwhelming if you have too many at the same time. Be sure to create your own internal system to manage all of your various ideas. Think of it as a filing system within your mind that prioritizes the ideas and decides which should be on the active list. Then go back and review the file every so often to ensure that you always have a project to work on.

4: Create A Plan And Stick To It

Once you have an idea, you need a plan. Once you have a plan, you need the resolve to stick to it. Create a timeline, mapping out key milestones and ensure that you stick to the plan. Think of each plan as a promise you are making to yourself so that each idea will actually see the light of day.

Section 6: Conclusion

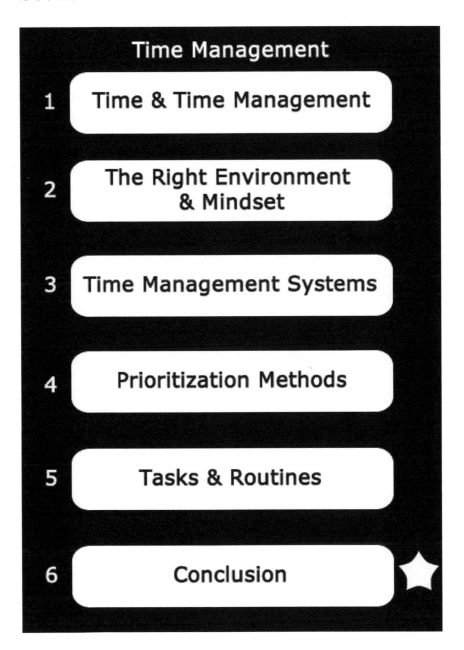

Time Management

1 Time & Time Management

2 The Right Environment & Mindset

3 Time Management Systems

4 Prioritization Methods

5 Tasks & Routines

6 Conclusion

45. Goal Setting & Time Management

Goal setting and time management are two different concepts, but they are practically inter-related and intertwined.

Time management would not be effective and achievable without goal setting.

Goal setting, for its part, needs effective time management skills for it to be successfully achieved.

Remember, when managing your time, the first thing you should attend to would be assessing or setting out your list of priorities. Doing so will enable you to carry out tasks that need to be carried out first.

It would be impossible for anyone to set priorities without first setting goals. Priorities are things that should be given primary and foremost focus and attention. The same applies to goals.

Priorities and goals are almost the same in that both are the ultimate targets and aims of each individual.

46. The Ultimate Time Management Tool

Congratulations! Throughout the book, you've been introduced to various proven techniques that will enable you to make the most of your time as you work to achieve your dreams.

The Ultimate Time Management Tool is the tool that works for you. Because our individual circumstances show an enormous variation it eventually comes down to you to choose a method that works best for you.

Personally I use a combination from various methods that help me make the best use of my time and to help me reach my goals. Keep in mind that my environment (I work mainly at home) and job (I am a writer) may ask for a different approach than yours.

I trust however, that you will be able to make the best choice to fit your needs perfectly.

Time management is the process of working to succeed. When we are working to succeed, we are reaching our goals. Celebrate your accomplishments!

47. How to Get in Contact

Well, you have reached the end of this book, but not the end of your learning. Please share with me your successes. I'd love to hear about them. I hope you enjoyed reading this book as much as I enjoyed creating it. You are already ahead of most people because you care enough to learn more. Now all you have to do is go out and use this knowledge. I would like to see you have tremendous success!

You can reach me by using the contact information you will find at http://www.raymond-le-blanc.com & http://twitter.com/raymondleblanc

My Personal Thank You!

I thank you for purchasing "Time Management Tips, Tools & Techniques " and would love to hear from you. If you enjoyed the information in this book, it would be much appreciated to hear what you think. So I encourage you to leave a quick review to let others know what you liked in this book.

Thank you for your help and time and look out for the other book in this series called: " Goal Setting Success Secrets."

http://www.amazon.com/Setting-Secrets-Revitalize-Achieving-ebook/dp/B00935MTJ8/

Author Raymond Le Blanc

Raymond Le Blanc is the author of several self help non-fiction books. He was born and raised in Kuala Lumpur, Malaysia before his family left for Europe.

Raymond holds a master's degree in economics and clinical psychology. Together with his wife Karin and their children, Raymond lives in a rural area of The Netherlands.

Bibliography
Books

Allen, David. Getting Things Done. New York: Penguin Books, 2001.

Babauta, Leo. The Power of Less. New York. Hyperion. 2009

Bradbury, Andrew. Develop your NLP Skills. London. Kogan. 2006

Bruce, Andy & Langdon, Ken. Simplify Your Life. New York. DK Publishing. 2001

Bruno, Dave. The 100 Thing Challenge. New York. HarperCollins. 2010

Canfield, Jack and Janet Switzer. How to Get From Where You Are to Where You Want to Be. New York: HarperCollins Publishers, 2007.

Covey, S. R., Merrill, A. R. & Merrill, R. R. (1994). "First Things First." New York: Fireside.

Covey, Stephen R. The Seven Habits of Highly Effective People: Restoring the Character Ethic. New York: Simon & Schuster, 1989.

Davenport, Liz. Order from Chaos: A Six-Step Plan for Organizing Yourself, Your Office, and Your Life. New York: Three Rivers Press, 2001.

Dilts, Robert. Verander Je Overtuigingen. Andromeda, 2006.

Dodd, Pamela and Doug Sundheim. The 25 Best Time Management Tools & Techniques: How to Get More Done Without Driving Yourself Crazy. Ann Arbor, MI: Peak Performance Press, Inc., 2005.

Ferriss, Timothy. The 4-Hour Workweek: Escape 9-5, Live Anywhere, and Join the New Rich. New York: Crown, 2007.

Forsyt, Patrick. 100 Great Time Management Ideas. Singapore. Marshall Cavendish. 2009

Grenier, Marc. GoalPro Success Guide. Initial Publishing, 2000.

Guillebeau, Chris. The Art of Non-Conformity. London. Perigee. 2011

Harris, Carol. NLP An Introductory Guide to the Art and Science of Excellence. Element Books, 2000.

Haynes, Marion E. Persoonlijk Tijdmanagement. Academic Service, 2000.

Hindle, Tim. Manage Your Time. New York. DK Publishing 1998

Joyner, Mark. Simpleology. The Simple Science of getting What you Want. New Jersey. John Wiley & Sons, 2007

Kelsey, Robert. What's Stopping You, Chichester. Capstone Publishing. 2011

Kievit-Broeze, Ineke E. Effectief Tijdbeheer. Handleiding voor praktisch time- en self-management. Schoonhoven: Academic Service, 1998.

Kustenmacher, Werner Tiki. Simplify Your Life. Munchen. Knauer. 2008

Linden, Anné and Kathrin Perutz. Mindworks: NLP Tools for Building a Better Life. Kansas City, MO: Andrews McMeel,1997.

Mancini, Marc. Time Management. Madison, WI: CWL Publishing Enterprises, Inc., 2003.

Millman, Dan. The Life You Were Born to Live: A Guide to Finding Your Life Purpose. H J Kramer,1993.

Pollar, Odette. Organizing Your Work Space, Revised Edition: A Guide to Personal Productivity. Mississauga, Ontario, Canada: Crisp Learning, 1998.

Seerup, Kevin, et al. GoalMaker. The Complete Goal Management System, Experience the Possibilities. Access Able Systems,1997.

Seiwert, Lothar J. Het 1+1 van Tijd-Management. Time/system,1988.

Seiwert, Lothar, Time-Management. Aartselaar. ZuidNederlandse Uitgevery 2002

Smith, Hyrum W. What Matters Most: The Power of Living Your Values. New York: Simon & Schuster, 2001.

Turkington, Carol A. Stress management for Busy People. McGraw-Hill,1998.

Vaklin, Shlomo, The Big Book of NLP, Inner Patch Publishing,2010

Web Pages

How the World's Richest 1% Get More Done by Working Less - And Less Hard, Too., http://www.simpleology.com/indexs16.php (2007-04-11)

Interactive Wheel of Life. http://www.jamuna.com/InteractiveWheel.swf (2007-04- 13)

"Law of Attraction." Wikipedia, http://en.wikipedia.org/wiki/Law_of_Attraction (2007-04-11)

Living Congruently, http://www.stevepavlina.com/blog/2005/02/living-congruently/ (2012-08-01)

NLP Meta Programs, http://www.nlpls.com/articles/metaPrograms.php (2012-08-01)

Personal "Energy Audit." http://ozpk.tripod.com/0000emotion (2007-04-11)

Seven NLP Meta-Programs for Understanding People, http://sourcesofinsight.com/seven-meta-programs-for-understanding-people/ (2012-08-01)

Simpleology 101 Review. http://www.soulselfhelp.com/simpleology-101.html (2007- 04-11)

Success Discoveries. http://www.successdiscoveries.com/ (2008-09-24)

The Science of Goal Achievement. http://www.ironmagazine.com/article177.html

Walker, Karen. http://www.karenwalkercoaching.com (2007-04-11)

Wheel of Life. http://www.rainbow-journey.org/cgi-bin/multiradar.pl (2007-04-11)

Worksheets to Help You Create Your Own Internet Lifestyle Plan, http://www.mymarketingcoach.com/goalworksheets.pdf (accessed November 19, 2011)

Audio

Allen, David. Ready for Anything: 52 Productivity Principles for Work and Life (Audio CD), Simon & Schuster Audio,2003.

Bliss, Edward C. Doing It Now (4 Pack) Cassette: How To Cure Procrastination And Achieve Your Goals In Twelve Easy Steps, Simon & Schuster Audio, 1987.

Morgenstern, Julie. Time Management from the Inside Out, Abridged edition, Simon & Schuster Audio, 2000.
How to Manage Priorities and Meet Deadlines (Audio Seminars) (Audio Cassette). Nightingale Conant, 1993.

Made in the USA
San Bernardino, CA
08 January 2013